# THE EGG MOON

BOOKS BY VON GOODWIN
The Lenten Moon
The Egg Moon
The Hunter's Moon
The Hitching Post of the Sun

VON GOODWIN WEBSITE
www.vongoodwin.com
This website contains additional products,
services, resources and links.

# THE EGG MOON

## LIVING THE QUESTION

### VON GOODWIN

**BALBOA.**
PRESS
A DIVISION OF HAY HOUSE

Balboa Press books may be ordered through booksellers or by contacting:

Balboa Press
A Division of Hay House
1663 Liberty Drive
Bloomington, IN 47403
www.balboapress.com
1-(877) 407-4847

Because of the dynamic nature of the Internet, any web addresses or
links contained in this book may have changed since publication and
may no longer be valid. The views expressed in this work are solely those
of the author and do not necessarily reflect the views of the publisher,
and the publisher hereby disclaims any responsibility for them.

The author of this book does not dispense medical advice or prescribe the use
of any technique as a form of treatment for physical, emotional, or medical
problems without the advice of a physician, either directly or indirectly. The
intent of the author is only to offer information of a general nature to help
you in your quest for emotional and spiritual well-being. In the event you use
any of the information in this book for yourself, which is your constitutional
right, the author and the publisher assume no responsibility for your actions.

Any people depicted in stock imagery provided by Thinkstock are
models, and such images are being used for illustrative purposes only.
Certain stock imagery © Thinkstock.

ISBN: 978-1-4525-3416-9 (sc)
ISBN: 978-1-4525-3437-4 (e)

Printed in the United States of America

Balboa Press rev. date:5/5/2011

Dedicated to:

Sharon Gammell

*As my mentor, she taught me to live life as a participant, not a victim.*

# PREFACE

*Most people live, whether physically, intellectually or morally, in a very restricted circle of their potential being. They make very small use of their possible consciousness and of their soul's resources in general, much like a man who, out of his whole bodily organism, should get into a habit of using and moving only his little finger.*

William James

Consciousness is thinking with awareness. And awareness is the realization that there is far more that is experienced than is perceived. Consciousness does not have a speed limit, the mind does. Biologically, the brain processes data from our multiple senses at 400 billion bits of information per second, but we are only aware of 2,000 bits at any one time. That is far less than one percent. In fact, it is 0.0000005% of what is sensed! Moreover, the mind processes information as images. And the rate at which that information is processed is 24 frames per second. We can only see in our brain what we're able to see, or are conditioned to see. In fact, we only see what we believe is possible, reducing the unbelievable to fantasy and illusion. Perhaps this explains why some of us that are more sensitive to the unconventional can see angels, paranormal entities and other realities. So, the question then becomes, what is it that one is experiencing that one is not seeing?

The reality is that there will always be something there that may not be perceived. And the focus then becomes on what is it that is most critical in discernment, and what is not? The Lenten Moon chronicled a tragic time for me and my sister with my Mother's death, one that presented a fork in the road with regards to reasoning and reckoning. The decision to become a victim, or to become a participant, was not clear in the beginning. Initially, the response was a natural one for Western thinking and that is to assume the role of one that had been harmed. And in doing so, exact a measure of vengeance. And the peril in doing that is to run the risk of being perpetually stuck in quack mire of self-inflicted guilt and pain; and hence to bear the label of victim.

The other option was to accept what had happened and to view death as a transition and not a final act. And in doing so, life then provides a series of interventions as if stepping stones on a dark path. With each placement of a foot, one anticipates a secure foundation on which to place the other. The Egg Moon, this book, describes several of those steps and the obvious benefits. What may not be so obvious are the actions that fashioned the interventions.

We are taught as children that good intentions shape one's life. And good intentions are not bad, good intentions are often not manifested into reality. That is, a wish, or a desire implies lack, or something someone does not have, and consequently what one may desire. In the daily course of one's life, noble thoughts are entertained. These thoughts are expressed in words and the words are followed by actions. So, our thoughts become words and our words become actions and actions become who we are.

It seems simple and straightforward to desire change in who

we are and what we do and far too often the terminology – the words – get in the way. A simple statement where one might say, "I want to be successful!" implies a current state of lack of success. And furthermore, the statement becomes a self fulfilling prophecy where the desire becomes the result; creating a type of inability to take action. So, to simply say, "I want…", is to have. That is, *to have* a desire for something and not that something.

In all of the examples provided in this book, the concept of *Conscious Language* was utilized, knowingly, or not. That is, the blending of expectation and gratitude created opportunities of learning and enlightenment. Whether it was the healing of the ruptured disk in my neck, or the finding of a lost book, each incident was preceded by an expectation. Just as science has now hypothesized that space is endless because of the human intent of expecting there to be more, and more space, so it is with living. One is either expecting more, or one is simply hoping there is more. Wanting and hoping creates a victim's existence, while expecting and gratitude enables one to become a participant and thus to experience more.

One's mind can be tricky. And what may seem to be harmless sayings such as, "Chocolate is to die for", or "I can't believe I am so stupid", or "I hope I don't get sick", or "You broke my heart" are limiting beliefs that have repercussions. And far too often we know from something deep within us that chocolate is not worth that price. And we know from a higher voice that frustration is often the source of self deprecation. And we know from a primeval sense that the cells that comprise the human body have their own consciousness and can provide their own healing. And yet, having an instinctive knowledge of this, we still succumb. Living a life being connected with the Source begins by having words that comes from your lips that reflect higher thoughts of who you really are. When we see ourselves as creators we then become aware that everything we do, and everything we say, and everything we think is part of a manifestation. And understanding this is a powerful tool in one's existence. It is necessary to become a participant in life. It defines one as creator.

The purpose of this writing is to provide a listing of awakenings. Moments and happenings that either provided flashes of enlightenment or occurrences that sowed slow-growing seeds of awareness. It is not intended to be a sequential accounting of a life, nor is it intended to be writing with heroes and villains. It is what it is; essays of discovery. I asked a select number of friends and associates to preview this writing. There were those that applauded the contents and found answers to very old questions and encouragement to make course corrections in living. And then there were those that didn't get it at all and that is okay. Even though I found extreme satisfaction in those I could help, those that I didn't assist meant it was simply not their time. One is not receptive until first there is a perceived need, it is the adage that one can lead a horse to water, but one cannot make it drink.

It is my hope that the words of this book captures the imagination of the reader and becomes a primer for those who are in search of a personal awakening; those that are living their questions.

# THE CRACK BETWEEN THE WORLDS

*We do not inherit the Earth from our Ancestors;*
*we borrow it from our Children.*
Indigenous Rights Quotes

The mountains seemed immutable, stalwarts guarding the gates of eternity. Their stoic confidence cut the wind, the clouds and the flight of the condor. As timeless sentinels of an endless process of life and living, the stone cliffs give a face to a name; a name the locals use to brand nature itself, Pachamama. And what seems to be a fixed world to the spiritually unconscious is but an illusion; change and cycles are constant. And it is here atop a peak that thrusts eight thousand feet above sea level, and within the walls of an ancient, abandoned city, a monument is found that chronicles the dynamics of change and cycles. The *Intiwatana* at Machu Picchu is carved from a massive stone, and is known as the *hitching post of the sun*. It is a carved rock pillar whose four corners are oriented toward the four cardinal points; north, south, east and west. And, as legend has it, an Incan shaman on the 21st day of June each year would ceremoniously tie one end of a rope to this hitching post and the other to a golden disc representing the sun. This ceremony dramatized the shaman's corralling of the sun to have it begin its return on the day of the winter solstice to the land of the Inca, and to announce the advent of the next growing season.

The tour group was led by a notable author and was given permission to enter the ruins at dawn. Fifty seven mystic travelers found their way to the site of the hitching post. Its positioning at the highest point of the ancient city made the panorama of shadows and ethereal clouds chilling. The Urubamba River winding its way through the Scared Valley of the Inca below hinted of an existence far beyond this place; this as if to symbolize a separation between the physical and the spiritual. And as one stands at the edge of the terracing surrounded by works of antiquity, encompassed by the forces of nature, and enveloped by the energy of those that were once there and still remain in spirit, there is a sense of being suspended between two dimensions.

The time between the predawn darkness and the appearance of the sun's first ray of light was described by the ancients as *the crack between the worlds*. This cusp provided heightened sensitivity to that side of humanness that was once considered an integral part of living, and is now considered by many to be suspicious and superstitious. And it was here I found myself suspended between many existences, thoughts and memories; between the physical and the spiritual, between the valley and the mountaintop.

The guide led a meditation at the *hitching post*. The cool morning air, the occasional sound of an exotic call of a distant bird and the sense that there were more in attendance than could be seen, made the ceremony tingling. The meditation focused on a single query. One that centered on what one may leave undone if one were to immediately depart the planet. With an extended period of silence, each took inventory of their lives and works. Then as if to provide a point of reference to ground one's thoughts, the suggestion was made to tie an end of one's spiritual rope to the *hitching post* and the other to the sun. The symbolic return of the sun would then announce the advent of a personal growing season. And it was at that time an overwhelming feeling of gratitude overcame me. And a sense of confidence ennobled me. And with a newfound calling of purpose and guidance in what I must do, I saw the answer in the stone walls that encircled me.

Hidden symbolisms in stone were constructed by the ancients to record a message and experience that would survive the ages. The Inca used quipu, a system of strings and knots, to record information that was important to their survival. And this system of *talking knots* was made of material that would not survive the ages. So, the Inca replicated the more important quipus in stonework at sacred sites. And that became the inspiration for me to chronicle events in my life; events that had proved to be providential. The quipu was equivalent to my verbally telling the tale of my growth, and the stones reflected a more permanent methodology in the written word. I envisioned that the sequence of events in my life mirrored the exactness of the stacked stones of Machu Picchu. And that the perfectly fitted joints of those stones reflected the elegance in timing of my events; and that defied explanation in both respects.

The full moon was still visible well after sunrise. This orb is called the Egg Moon and marks the beginning of spring; a time of new beginning and growth. It is a time that signals the end of long, cold nights and the gradual lengthening and warming of days. It is a time to tend to activities that will produce fruit and the necessities in living. It is a time to become reacquainted with one's connection to the source. It is a time of change. And this celestial occurrence symbolized an awakening and an evolution to a place where thoughts are based in awareness; seeing more than what is visible.

The following is what some may call coincidence. It is far more than coincidence, or chance; it is an orchestration. Strangely, as you will soon discover, the impetus for what happens comes from within as intent and is mirrored in the physical world as reality. And oddly enough, my reason for chronicling these events is to provide an opportunity for others to experience what most recognize as twists-of-fate are in fact conscious creation.

# A MOST TRAGIC EVENT

*There is nothing more tragic than to find an individual*
*bogged down in the length of life, devoid of breadth.*
Martin Luther King, Jr.

I was where I needed be, at a time that was meant to be. The idea of a better time and place had no meaning as there is no such thing as coincidence. A feeling of relief rushed over me. A sweet surrender comforted me. It was as if a tired fugitive had been caught, and the anxiety of running and hiding was replaced with acceptance. And with acceptance the fear of being exposed was gone. For the first time, in a long time, I was at baseline – at a point where what was experienced as a tragedy now appeared to be a tutorial to a higher calling. It was a lesson that was paid by a life, and a message that was announced by an alarming accident. As the ending of a physical life announces the beginning of another existence, so it was with this transition. It was a conversion from a perspective of life based on fear to one based on love.

I awoke to the hissing sound of escaping steam and the smell of engine coolant and oils. Months earlier my efforts to bring those accountable for a preventable death had ended with a declaration of innocence. A jury of unfocused peers had deliberated for minutes to deliver an eternal decision. The blurry image of the traffic light flashed its colors as the muffled sound of bystanders competed for my attention. Things happened in slow motion; movements, sounds and thoughts were surreal. The last thing I remembered were the sounds of a car horn and screeching tires, and then a crushing pain in my chest. It was then I lost consciousness.

There were times when I would plunge into a state of mind that seemed like a trance and relive aspects of the thirty one day ordeal. It was an ordeal that blended a patient's confidence in a doctor's medical ability and disclosure with a medical provider's deceit and arrogance. And that lethal alchemy created the poison that took my mother's life. Tonight my focus was on the morning of her death, a day where minutes were fleeting, and yet eternal. Moments whose memories would last a lifetime, and seconds whose duration was far too brief.

*\*\**

The three hours of sleep was not much of an escape as I hurried to ready myself for a long day. It was to be a day of medical interventions to correct a series of misfortune. Misfortune that had begun a month earlier with what was described to me as an unremarkable heart attack and subsequent cardio arterial bypass grafts, and was culminating with a corrective procedure utilizing an experimental drug. Wrestling with tasks that were usually performed in a semiconscious state, these tasks were now dispiriting exercises.

These movements caused a level of aggravation that caused tears and expletives to flow. It was as if I were physically impaired. Dropping my toothbrush into the toilet, falling in the shower and popping buttons from my clothing were occurrences that on any given day would be a comedy of errors and brushed away as clumsiness. But today was not a typical day. With one eye on the clock, and the other on the hotel door, I was at long last ready to rush to the cardiac surgical floor of the hospital.

Making my way toward the door, while still gathering myself, my departure was interrupted by a command made by my companion. The order was a demand to slow down and show some consideration for one's spouse and wait. Ordinarily the request would have been an appropriate accommodation. Today, however, was not an ordinary day. The request came with a scolding that ten minutes would not matter and we could then go together as a family. And opting to concede a few minutes to avoid generating rage, I succumbed to what I considered then to be bullying and waited. Turning quickly to look at the clock, I had fifteen minutes to get to Mother's room before she would be taken to the surgical suite for a second operation and an attempt to perform a risky, triple bypass surgery.

As I arrived, the nurses were removing her from the room. I leaned and kissed her. Taking her hand, I walked alongside the gurney as we passed the nurse's station. I had grown to know the staff. Their names and faces were familiar and comforting. They wished mother and me well with words of encouragement and uplifted thumbs. Turning the corner, two large doors opened. Placed above the opening was a sign that limited entry to hospital staff, and verbal instructions were then made by the nurse to say goodbye, and that I could not go further. The simple statement had the sound of a tragic myth, a tale that could not possibly be happening. Movements occurred in slow motion as I kissed her once again and whispered goodbye. And that was the last time I saw her alive.

The anguish in having been delayed by my own clumsiness made me hate myself, at times. And the self-centered request of my partner deprived me of precious moments, and could never be forgotten. Both haunted me. My last moments with the person who knew me best slipped away. And the only person that could chronicle my life was gone. And I wasted the last opportunity to share that lifetime of memories in a final loving glance. To share one more intimate thought in a spoken word and to hear the voice that had comforted me so many times. To simply say thank you for all that she had done for me. And it was those feelings that consumed my attention as I ignored a stop light and struck another car.

I regained and lost consciousness at the hospital, slipping in and out of cognizance. I recalled hearing someone mention that I was the only one injured in the accident. This was a wakeup call that it was time to give my life a new direction, and the emotion of the incident moved me toward a time of reflection. And the horrific accident was the alarm that would provide the motivation.

I lay there with my eyes closed. I did not know with any degree of certainty if what I sensed around me was reality, or an orchestration of my making, or if the two were one in the same. The beeps and clicks of the medical equipment proved to be hypnotic as I recalled the last day of mother's life. The surgeon had made bold assertions that the risky surgery he was scheduled to perform was well within his abilities as a doctor. And, even though, as I later learned, he and his staff had never performed a surgery using leech saliva as an anticoagulant, he nonetheless stated he had been trained at a well respected North Carolina medical school. This, too, was not true. To compound the recklessness of the surgery, the need for the second heart surgery was the result of an undiagnosed allergy to Heparin. This allergy caused the first bypasses to clot and the surgeon failed to recognize the symptoms.

I closed my eyes and remembered the last time I saw Mother's body.

\*\*\*

The cabin of the plane shook violently. The confusion of the moment created a panic that caused young and old to grapple for available oxygen masks. Screams of terror and faces of desperation were outward displays of abject fear as each passenger knew that death was close at hand. A violent end whose imminence robbed each of the most compassionate final act afforded to even the most undeserving among us, the opportunity to simply say goodbye to a loved one. And those that were facing this experience were common folk; anyone's sister or brother, son or daughter, wife or husband. And as I sat there as a member of this group, I was overcome with a sensation of complete serenity and awareness. Fear was not with me.

The plane crashed. And with the flash of a brilliant light and the sound of a muffled explosion, my body floated in complete silence and darkness. Weightless and relaxed, cognizant and expectant, I waited for my next opportunity. The next opportunity to experience what was previously known to me as life. I did not know when I would transition, or to what time or place; I simply knew it would happen. I had been here before. It was then a conspicuous point of light appeared and grew larger as it streaked toward me, or I toward it. The point of light was a portal, an opening through which I was drawn. My transition had begun.

At that moment, the pastor presiding at my Mother's funeral service slammed his Bible onto the pulpit, and then instructed the attendants to close the casket. The sound of the Scripture making contact with the wooden podium startled me from my trance. The dream of the plane crash and my death had occurred the night before, and for reasons unknown to me my consciousness was directed to the dream at a time that would seem most inappropriate. Why would I daydream at a time like this?

It was as though something wanted me to sense the peace

and purpose that death provides, and that an ending is in fact a beginning. At that instance the pastor proclaimed with his arms extended that we can all take comfort in knowing that she is in a better place, in a heavenly place, awaiting her reward. It was then a most compelling thought entered my consciousness, awaiting her reward, or awaiting her transition – could the two be one in the same?

We then stood as the throng sang a hymn. It was a song of celebration, not one of eternal separation. The number in attendance stressed the sanctuary as the standing-room-only crowd spilled into the foyer and onto the street. The sheer volume of the vocal salute overshadowed the musical instruments and created a chill in my body. The lyrics heralded victory in Jesus as the pall bearers rolled the honored to the awaiting hearse.

A procession of mourners followed the lead car to the cemetery. The March wind and rain made the elements unbearable, and its effects mirrored my innermost feelings. Comfort was an ephemeral harbor as both the turmoil within and the storms without created a dire symmetry. Nowhere could I go for refuge, and there was nothing I could do to remove the sting of death.

The six men chosen to place the casket onto the canvas straps that spanned the grave opening tread through mud of the recently unearthed plot. Each had been a close friend of the family and each performed the duty as a final act of respect. The pastor read familiar passages from the Bible. A verse from Corinthians that promised the dead in Christ will rise again, and a passage from Psalms that mentioned walking through the valley of the shadow of death. Those in attendance offered up their encouragement and approval with frequent Amen's. And then the pastor instructed the funeral director to release the locks on the canvas straps. The casket slowly descended in to the red clay of Bibb County as did my heart. And there her body remains to this day.

My sense of loss did not diminish. And her death on the day of the Lenten Moon had added symbolism. For the ancient Christians, the rising of the Lenten Moon signaled the beginning of a time of mournful respect for the death of Christ at the hands of the Romans. And it marked the beginning of a time of grief and confusion for me. Thirty one days of decisions and second-guessing tilled the soil of doubt and produced its harvest of self inflicted guilt. My heart grappled with many uncertainties as I attempted to find closure. I looked for ways to punish myself and those who were responsible for mother's death.

It was at that moment the nurse whispered in my ear that it was time to rest. Struggling to open my eyes, I saw her inject into the IV a substance that made my senses move in slow motion. Watching her lips move and hearing nothing, I closed my eyes to my hurt, both emotional and physical and opened them to a time of insightful tranquility.

The drug that caused the closure of my consciousness to the finite, physical world opened a new door to an extraordinary world of possibilities. To a world where possibilities exist as waves of potential and become singular by one's observation. The sights, sounds and smells of the hospital room were pushed away. And in the place of the familiar was that of the primal, that aspect of existing which makes sense of one's experience – the inner voice. And, as if I were guided by an unseen raconteur, the years of grief unfolded before me. Experiences that were once dismissed as trivial were played out before me with added emphasis. Lost in those experiences were lessons and guidance that would prove to be a type of providence, and were by no means a coincidence.

The apparent coincidence of fallen angels, found books, a

single word, chance meetings, strange places, guardian angels and new acquaintances were orchestrations of natural and divine laws. I heard a voice that said to expect the remarkable: This story of my awakening.

# THE FALLEN

*There were giants in the earth in those days; and also after that, when the sons of God came in unto the daughters of men, and they bear children to them, the same became mighty men which were of old, men of renown.*

Genesis 6: 4

The small wooden framed structure had been an iconic presence for almost 200 years. The walls have been privy to generations of church members that have worshipped within its confines since 1827. Obvious architectural nuances dated the building as a historic monument. The edifice is supported by a foundation of stone pillars that are placed at close intervals. And between the pillars is an open crawl space that exposes the under-flooring to temperature variants that makes it next to impossible to effectively heat and cool the sanctuary. The windows are paned with a special glass, and upon close examination one can see small pockets of air; some call it Depression glass.

A steeple that cradles a bell calls the community to a time of worship. And its deep tones falls on deaf ears as the majority of seats remain empty on any given Sunday. The steps, quarried from the nearby Cahaba River, leads to the front door. The set of steps are old and worn and unstable. The floor creaks as if to proclaim the age of the building and the oak pews induce moans from those in attendance, as if to remind the worshippers of their aging. This symbolic give and take seems to be a constant in nature, reminding me of the connectedness that exist in creation and the cycles it represents.

The annual memorial service in late May to honor the deceased that are interned in the adjoining cemetery taxed the resources of the facility. Air conditioning provided minimal relief as the heat and humidity of central Alabama took its toll. It was the first memorial service since mother's death. And I was more interested in publicly representing her with my attendance than I was with the details of the church service. Battling the elements using the service program as a makeshift fan, my attention drifted to areas of my life beyond the walls of the sanctuary. It was then the pastor began her sermon. It was a homily that referenced a familiar biblical tale. It was the story of Noah and the flood; Genesis, Chapter Six.

Reading from the scriptures, the pastor paused to compose herself after reading a key verse. The pause created a silence that I found to be deafening with respect to what had been stated. As a child I had heard this story many times. And my focus had always been on the Ark and its contents. The parading of animals, two-by-two, and the riding-out of the forty day storm was at that time the focus of my attention. Never had I contemplated the verse that mentioned giants, or the reference to them being mighty men of renown. Who were these men? My mind raced with ideas and possibilities. On one hand, I was tempted to dismiss the tale as nonsense and on the other something seemed to suggest there was more to the story. After the service, I stopped at a Barnes and Noble on my way to the airport. I had to know more.

\*\*\*

As an adult I was conditioned to think rationally, or so it seemed to me. One did not accept the mythology of any culture, or religion, as a complete source of fundamental facts. And the notion that giants, floods and spirit beings existed had the sound of fantasy and fiction. The premise that sons of God took human women as wives and produced offspring was farfetched and ridiculous. And that the offspring were superhuman in size with exceptional physical ability and possessed supernatural powers was, well, the storylines of any seamy tabloid.

Set aside the fact that the source of this information by the most critical of standards is beyond reproach. And that the Bible in other respects gives an accurate geopolitical account of the ancient world. Then to presume some aspects, for convenience sake, must have been inserted as a joke, or as a concoction of an overly vivid imagination, is inconsistent with that which we know so well. How was one expected to trust selected tenets as absolute, and discard others as folklore? Certainly any thinking person could discern fact from fabrication, but how was one to know which was which. Or, could it be simply a matter of discarding that which we find unfamiliar, or uncomfortable; a convenient accommodation to not be troubled with that we find challenging or disturbing.

There were two irruptions of spirit beings; one prior to the Great Flood, and one after. Their appearance on earth prior to the flood which occurred in 2348 B.C. affected God's decision in destroying the inhabitants of the earth. Because of their impiety, all life was endangered, except for Noah and his family. The Bible states that God saw their wickedness and that their thoughts were continuously evil and that the earth was filled with violence. And after the flood, the spirit beings once again interacted with humans. Picking up where they were interrupted, the *fallen ones* continued to produce offspring with humans, and more.

Biblical passages and ancient art suggest an incredible mixing of human and animal DNA that resulted in experiments in nature that God found extremely vile. Experiments in genetic engineering that produced half-human and half-reptile, or half-bird, or half-something are depicted in artwork as interacting in common place settings with humans. Some historical apologists offer the explanation of *over active* imaginations, or that the depictions are symbolic, even though few, if any, symbolic explanations are presented. This influence and trafficking of life affected politics and genetics for centuries.

The *sons of God* married the *daughters of men* and produced children. These children were called Nephilim, which means *fallen ones*. The story of Goliath of Gath is told time, and again, with little attention to the application of detail. Goliath stood over thirteen feet in height; twice the height of a door opening and weighed over six hundred pounds. Og, another giant, and King of Bashan, required a bed that was over eighteen feet in length and eight feet in width – a bed the size of a sports utility vehicle. Goliath and Og were the children of the sons of God. And, the sons of God were the fallen angels that were cast out of the presence of the Almighty for their mutinous acts. The leader of this group of fallen angels was Lucifer, who was also called the *shining one* and *the morning star.*

Lucifer's intent in devising this interaction with humans was to derail God's plan. Lucifer's intention to contaminate the human species with alternative genetics was to bring about human extinction. And with the extinction of humankind, there would not be a woman to bring forth the seed to destroy Lucifer. God's plan to undo the damage Lucifer had orchestrated when he tempted Eve to eat the fruit of the tree of Knowledge is summarized in the book of Genesis Chapter 3, Verse 15. God told the Serpent, Lucifer:

*"And I will put enmity between you and the woman; and between your seed and her seed; it will crush your head and you will bruise his heel."*

The seed of a woman would ultimately destroy Lucifer, a fitting end in that he corrupted Eden by tempting woman. And the crucifixion was the final blow to his head. Although the Messiah would ultimately surrender his life, the altruistic act was but a mere bruising of the heel which is indicated as a superficial wound. Christ would nonetheless rise from the dead. And, Lucifer, and the fallen angels, would no longer be permitted to interact with humans as they had in times past.

Physical representations of the Nephilim still exist to this day. Hieroglyphs and drawings depicting the mixing of human and animal features were not the over active imagination of artists. The art works were factual representations of genetic manipulation by the sons of God. Drawings of human bodies with bird heads, human heads with feline bodies; all were represented interacting in everyday settings with humans.

Lucifer and his fallen angels were with God at the foundation of creation. Lucifer was described as the Morning Star, and the angels were referred to as *The Stars of Heaven*. God communicating with Job said:

> *Where were you when I laid the earth's foundations? Tell me if you have understanding. Who marked off its dimensions? Surely you know. Who stretched a measuring line across it? On what were its footings set, or who laid its cornerstone? When the morning stars sang together and all the sons of God shouted for joy.* Job 38:4-7.

Another reference to Lucifer is found in Isaiah 14:12.

*How you have fallen from Heaven, O Morning Star,*
*son of the dawn.*

My attention was drawn to the large number of references to the heavens, namely the stars. Lucifer's attempt to ascend beyond God, and his ultimate demotion in being cast down to earth, suggested a physical descent from a celestial origin. And, his nickname referencing the most prominent star in the night sky was intriguing. The word Nephilim means fallen ones; fallen from what? Fallen from grace, or fallen from the sky. References to sons of God shouting and the Morning Stars singing were too coincidental to ignore. Could there be more to this, human history and the apparent connection to the stars?

There is an undeniable consistency in worldwide belief in certain supposed myths; belief that conventional wisdom would dismiss as fanciful imaginings of shamans and clerics. Most cultures have a story of creation, and the existence, or promise of a redeemer that incorporates a storyline of a virgin birth initiated by supernatural intervention. Most cultures share a tale of a great flood. Most cultures have an undeniable connection to the heavens, whether it is a star in the east, a cloud by day or a pillar of fire at night for guidance, a story told within the zodiac, or an affinity to a cluster of stars called the Pleiades. A common theme in the orchestra of human experience is our connection to the stars. And a phrase in this ancient fugue is recorded by the Sumerians in the tale of the Annunaki.

Six thousand year old Sumerian Cuneiform tablets that have been deciphered record historical events that date back 450,000 years. This information predates Biblical history by well over

445,000 years, one hundred times the length of time recorded in the Bible. The tablets tell a tale of celestial beings from a planet named Nibiru. This planet traverses our solar system taking 3,600 years to orbit the sun. The inhabitants of this planet are called the Annunaki which means *those who came from heaven to earth*.

Sumerian cosmology suggests that Nibiru is the twelfth member of the solar system. The counted members include the nine planets, the sun, the earth's moon and Nibiru. Their knowledge of the nine planets is recorded two thousand years prior to modern astronomy. The Sumerians knowledge of Pluto, for example, predates that of modern man by thousands of years. Pluto was *re-discovered* in 1930 by Clyde W. Tombaugh. And the Sumerians numbered the planets from Pluto to the Mercury suggesting a perspective from beyond the solar system, as if the planets were exits on an interstellar highway.

The origin of the earth and the asteroid belt that lies between Mars and Jupiter was the result of a collision, or near collision, of Nibiru and the planet Tiamat. The Annunaki survived the collision and came to earth and genetically engineered the human species. The mixing of Homo Erectus DNA with that of the Annunaki produced slaves to work the mines for necessary minerals required by *those who came from heaven to earth*.

The 3,600 year orbit of Nibiru places the return of the planet near earth around 2012. This orbit is approximately one-seventh of the 25,625 Mayan Long Calendar-count that represents *5 World Ages*. The last passing of Nibiru near the earth was in 1649 BC and coincided with a number of natural disasters, including the eruption of Thera. The eruption was one the most powerful in the past 10,000 years and contributed to the fall of the Minoan Civilization, and is believed to have affected Atlantis.

Information from the library of Ashurbanipal indicates there was an uncharacteristic explosion of technology and scientific knowledge in Sumer at the time of the Annunaki. The Annunaki were related to the Biblical Nephilim. The Nephilim, the gods, were superior to the Annunaki. And humans were inferior to both. The need for minerals, particularly gold for its superior conductivity, necessitated the development of a mining industry. This was an industry that was conducted by the Nephilim as managers and the Annunaki as laborers. As the records suggest, the Annunaki became disgruntled with the arduous tasks and the slave-like treatment at the hands of the Nephilim. Arguments and wars between the two factions were common place. And the *evil wind* referred to in the *Lament for Ur* suggests superior weaponry; nuclear weaponry may have been utilized to destroy Ur. Negotiations resulted in a resolution; an agreement that involved the utilization of genetic engineering.

The Nephilim and the Annunaki agreed to combine the DNA of Homo Erectus with that of their own to create an intelligent, trainable species to carry out their mining activities. Humankind was created, and selected members of this hybrid species were *groomed* to be the go-betweens; managers of the human slaves and subjects to the Nephilim. This *grooming* of the human-kings produced a highly skilled and equipped superhuman. And it was this superhuman that possessed the knowledge, skills and talents that one associates with the leaders of the ancient world and their supernatural abilities.

As in the case of Moses' encounter with the Pharaoh of Egypt when he demanded the release of the Israelites and asked Aaron to cast his rod before King. The rod transformed into a snake. And Pharaoh commanded his priests to perform the same feat. It was then Aaron's snake consumed the snakes of Pharaoh's ministers.

Regardless of who won the encounter, both were equally skilled, and equipped, with magic.

The blending of the two stories places a hierarchy of the Nephilim at the top representing the offspring of the supernatural fallen angels. The next in line would have been the Annunaki that were superiorly skilled and talented extraterrestrials from Nibiru. Following the Annunaki are the genetically engineered humans that were created from Homo erectus. And then Homo erectus at the bottom of the pecking order. Scattered throughout the process are experiments that are chronicled in writing, and art, that represents the stuff of which myths are created.

The fusing of the Biblical story of the fallen angels and their copulation with human women with the Sumerian account of genetic engineering may be inappropriate. To describe two *myths* whose end results are essentially identical is the intent. And both describe entities from space that interacted with humans to produce unusual offspring is a similarity that cannot be ignored.

As incredible as it may sound, belief in the existence of these demigods would be far easier to accept if one would step forward and demonstrate its powers. Where are they, and if they are not here, where did they go?

As Tacitus, the prestigious Roman historian writes:

> *The doors of the inner shrine were suddenly thrown open, and a voice of more than mortal tone was heard to cry that the Gods were departing. At the same instant there was a mighty stir as of departure.*

The gods departed the night the temple located in Jerusalem was destroyed. Their leaving the planet was foretold by Christ as he told his disciples:

*And Jesus went out, and departed from the temple: and his disciples came to him for to shew him the buildings of the temple. And Jesus said unto them, See ye not all these things? Verily I say unto you, there shall not be left one stone upon another that shall not be thrown down. And as he sat upon the Mount of Olives, the disciples came unto him privately, saying; tell us, when shall these things be? And what will be the sign of thy coming, and the end of the world? Matthew 24:1 – 3*

And Christ answered when the destruction of the temple would occur:

*Verily I say unto you, <u>This</u> generation shall not pass, till all these things be fulfilled. Matthew 24:34*

The date of Christ's crucifixion is believed to be April 3, A.D. 33. And the Bible references the duration of a generation as forty years, Psalms 95:10. So, the disciples were told by Christ that those hearing his words could also witness the destruction of the temple and the end of their world. And the temple was destroyed in 70 A.D., less than forty years later.

*And then shall appear the sign of the Son of man in heaven: and then shall all the tribes of the earth mourn, and they shall see the Son of man coming in the clouds of heaven with power and great glory. And he shall send his angels with a great sound of a trumpet, and they shall gather together his elect from the four winds, from one end of heaven to the other. Matthew 24:30, 31*

Could this have been God's final interaction with humankind? Could this be why my prayers seemingly go unanswered?

I felt as though God had abandoned me in moment when I was in great need. And to compound the feelings, for God to have abandoned mother was inexplicable. Circumstances seemed to have orchestrated a series of events that affected my thoughts. Alone, and without recourse, I sensed a need to turn inward for my answers and it was there I found more questions.

In a classic form of denial, I had avoided any and all contact with what would have reminded me of the worse time of my life. And the mixing of anger and bargaining set into motion a legal option to hold those that I considered guilty to be exposed for what they were, disingenuous. The stages of grief that had gotten me to this point had also set the stage for the next. The coincidence of a sermon that casually mentioned Biblical giants, an apparent demigod exodus from the planet, and a found book describing the Dark Ages did little to encourage me. And the next step of grief was all too real; depression. I needed a personal renaissance. I had to rediscover myself.

# A FOUND BOOK

*Don't believe what your eyes are telling you.*
*All they show is limitation.*
*Look with your understanding,*
*find out what you already know,*
*and you'll see the way to fly.*
Richard Bach

With the passing of a day, and the exposure of a new insight, my attention was redirected from the pain and anger of the past. It seemed with every turn in my life circumstance was laying a needed *distraction* at my feet. The needed distractions ultimately proved to be steps of an intervention that would not only assist in my recovery, but would take me far beyond my level of understanding prior to the tragic event. At that time it seemed extremely coincidental – the random series of findings and discoveries – and in retrospect a deep sense of gratitude seems more appropriate for the miracles strewn along my pathway.

As the sermon at the memorial service sparked further investigation that led to my discovery of fallen sons of God and displaced aliens, so it was with how human events of a thousand years past affects my thinking today. That legacy of deep seated roots of the past are still bearing dark fruits in the present.

Culture is the sum total of ways of living built up by a group of human beings, and transmitted from one generation to another. This transference of information and tradition is the source of folklore and religion, and serves far more than just the need for a good bedtime story or a word of encouragement during difficult times. It is necessary for those that need a predictable existence to live in comfort and acceptance. And it should not be surprising that the culture in which we live affects the way we manage our lives. In fact, until we understand that premise we are eternally put away in that existence; buried in a way of thinking that at times limits our abundance. And it serves a metaphor for a much deeper existence; that of a level of being that is invisible to the naked eye, but whose effects are experienced with each passing moment.

Culture affects the individual by shaping one's values, beliefs and deeply held assumptions. Those characteristics are wrapped up into what are considered norms. And norms of the Western world are centered on possessions. The need to have possessions necessitates practices that supply those needs. And in a tragic irony, in the Western world, *need* is defined as that which one does not have, or that which one is afraid of losing. Regardless, neither is truly required.

The migration to the temporal of Western culture has had far greater consequence than long work hours, unscrupulous tactics and stress-centered lives. It has forced an abandonment of an aspect of humanness that is as much a part of each of us as our name; our intuitiveness. To fully understand the culture in which we now live, we must first learn how we arrived at where we are today.

A found book, retrieved from the seatback of a Continental flight bound for Bakersfield, California, planted a seed that opened my eyes to a fundamental concept: One cannot correct an error in the same mental state in which it was created. And to understand one's mental state, one must understand the origins of beliefs and values. Often this requires understanding the soil in which culture is grown.

The revelation that science and spirituality can coexist is farfetched to some. The split occurred over 1,500 years ago, and the Western world is still reeling from the effects of the Dark Ages. It was a time when the surrender to abject mysticism muddied the waters of reason, and created both a panic based on fear of the unexplained and a naivety based on eagerness to hear answers, any answer that had promise of relief.

## The Fear

A Roman merchant ship docked at the southern most mooring at Ostia Antica, a port near Rome. The vessel was a Carvel designed ship with smooth-sided wooden planks fitted edge to edge over a frame and sealed with calking. The ship builders of the Mediterranean constructed their vessels in this manner because they had saws and could make square-cut planks, unlike the craftsmen of Northern Europe that overlapped the planks. The carvel-type ships suffered a serious drawback, though, in that they were difficult to make water-tight and water constantly seeped in. Their advantage was that they could be made to any length to maximize the cargo hold of the vessel. And the size of the cargo is what interested the Romans and their desire for excess and opulence.

The escutcheon is the part of the ship that displays the name of the vessel. And this ship proudly listed the name Proserpina. Proserpina was the Roman Goddess of the Underworld. The vessel was large, and its cargo of Ivory from the west coast of Africa was destined to satisfy the appetite for Roman greed. The cargo was stored on the lowest deck called the lastage, a room specifically designed to hold trade. The design of the ship caused frequent leakage and a fardage, an elevated flooring kept the goods dry. It was there, beneath the fardage, the rats hid as stowaways. And without any conscious thought on their part, the infected fleas that carried the plague lay concealed in their fur.

Docked at Ostia Antica, the rats made their way from the lastage up the companionway to the hawsehole, an opening through which the rope that moored the ship to the dock was passed. Using the rope as an escape path, the rats and their stowaways found their way to shore, to Rome and Europe, and the world. Proserpina, the Goddess of the Underworld had delivered her cargo.

The rats had poor vision, and their sight was limited to certain colors and distance. Their senses of hearing, touch and smell on the other hand were quite sensitive. The rats took indirect paths to their destinations, stealthily making their way amongst humankind. Their preferences were routes that permitted their whiskers to touch the surroundings. This sensory application coupled with their poor vision was akin to the blind finding their way with walking canes. And to enhance this ability their senses of hearing and smell were acute. Hearing and communicating at frequencies higher than that of humans gave them added security in avoiding human contact. Humans simply could not hear the tones of the rodents as they communicated in complete concealment. And their sense of smell provided a sightless panorama of their world. Transporting the infected fleas while stealthily avoiding man was little problem for rattus rattus.

The oriental rat flea that rode the backs of the rats had two eyes, yet it could only see very bright light. The flea's mouth had two functions: one for squirting saliva of partly digested blood into the bite, and one for sucking up blood from the host. This process mechanically passed pathogens that caused diseases.

The fleas smelled exhaled carbon dioxide from humans and animals, and would jump rapidly to the source to feed on the newly found host. The fleas were wingless so they could not fly, but they could jump long distances with the help of small powerful legs. The flea's leg consisted of four parts. The part that is closest to the body is the coxa. Next are the femur, tibia and tausus. With four joints, the leverage needed to propel their bodies was more than adequate to quickly move about. The flea used its legs to jump up to 200 times its own body length. It can also jump about 130 times its own height.

There were three forms of the Black Death transmitted two ways. The septicemic and bubonic plague were transmitted by direct contact with a flea, while the pneumonic plague was transmitted through airborne droplets of saliva coughed up by bubonic or septicemic infected humans.

The bubonic and septicemic plague was transmitted by the bite of an infected flea. Fleas, humans, and rats served as hosts for the disease. The bacteria Yersinia Pestis multiplied inside the flea blocking the flea's stomach causing it to be very hungry. The flea would then start voraciously biting a host. Since the feeding tube to the stomach was blocked, the flea was unable to satisfy its hunger. As a result, it continued to feed in frenzy. During the feeding process, infected blood carrying the plague bacteria flowed into the human's wound. The plague bacteria now had a new host. The flea soon starved to death.

The pneumonic plague was transmitted differently than the other two forms. It was transmitted through droplets sprayed from the lungs and mouth of an infected person. In the droplets were the bacteria that caused the plague. The bacteria entered the lungs through the windpipe and started attacking the lungs and throat.

The bubonic plague was the most commonly seen form of the Black Death; three out of four died from its effects. The symptoms were enlarged and inflamed lymph nodes around the arm pits, neck and groin. The term *bubonic* refers to the characteristic bubo or enlarged lymphatic gland. Victims were subject to headaches, nausea, aching joints, fever, vomiting, and a general feeling of illness. Symptoms took up to seven days to appear.

The pneumonic plague was the second most commonly seen form of the Black Death. The pneumonic and the septicemic plague were probably seen less than the bubonic plague because the victims often died before they could reach other places, this was caused by the inefficiency of transportation. The mortality rate for the pneumonic plague was nine of ten that contracted the disease; if treated today the mortality rate would be less than one in ten. The pneumonic plague infected the lungs. Symptoms included slimy sputum tinted with blood. Sputum is saliva mixed with mucus exerted from the respiratory system. As the disease progressed, the sputum became free flowing and bright red. Symptoms took up to seven days to appear.

The septicemic plague was the rarest form of all. Death was a certainty; even today there is no treatment. Symptoms were a high fever and skin turning deep shades of purple due to hyper-coagulation of the blood. In its most deadly form this condition, which is an over active protein that promotes clotting, can cause a victims skin to turn dark purple. The Black Death got its name from the deep purple, almost black discoloration. Victims usually died the same day symptoms appeared. In some cities, as many as 800 people died every day.

One was either sick, or knew someone who was. And the

effects of the epidemic created panic, or apathy. One was either too anxious as to what tomorrow held in store for them or, there was no hope for the future at all. The pandemic affected more than the bodies of the infected, it weakened the resolve of a culture and the way of life.

The economy was probably hit the hardest of all the aspects of Europe. The biggest problem was that valuable artisan skills disappeared when large numbers of the working class died. Therefore, those who had skills became even more valuable than the rich people. The society structure began to change giving formally poor laborers more freedom of expression. The peasants and artisans demanded higher wages. Serfs seeking liberation from tilling their lord's land were told by decree and statue to return to their master's duties.

The poor people saw so much death they wanted to enjoy life. Serfs began to leave their land and not engage in the planting of crops. Unattended crops and stray animals died of starvation because of the lack of care. Several species of domesticated animals began to roam the forests of Europe. Farming communities became rare.

The lack of sufficient law enforcement personnel promoted lawlessness. People called Bechini pillaged homes, murdering and raping people. They dressed in red robes with red masks, and only their eyes showed. The horror of the Black Death had taken on a new victim, the economy.

One of the groups that suffered the most was the Christian church. It lost prestige, spiritual authority, and leadership over the people. The church promised cures, treatment, and an explanation for the plague. They said it was God's will, but the reason for this awful punishment was unknown. People wanted answers, but the priests and bishops didn't have any. The clergy abandoned their

Christian duties and fled. People prayed to God and begged for forgiveness. After the plague ended, angry and frustrated villagers started to revolt against the church. The survivors were also enraged at doctors, who didn't cure patients, but said they could.

The combination of an epidemic and the absence of leadership created an atmosphere of fear and blame. The sources once trusted with having the answers to life's problems were suddenly locked-jawed and without credible response. Miracles were no-show occurrences and twenty five million deaths later, Europe, and much of Asia, was decimated.

There are those that believe that the pandemic of the Black Death was the catalyst for the Dark Ages, and there are others that hold to other contributing factors. A far reaching drought occurred that exposed a large portion of Eastern Europe to hunger and starvation. Nemea, Greece was the site of an archeological dig that unearthed a dried river bed, and remnants of a village that left telltale signs of a natural disaster. A team of scientists excavating deep into the bed of the small Nemea River which runs through the site made an unexpected discovery. A much larger, older river bed was discovered that had completely run dry during the first half of the 6$^{th}$ century A.D. Further discovery provided evidence of numerous wells that had been dug and used for a short time.

Nemea was totally destroyed by invading Slavs in 585 A.D. Although evidence suggests the community had been in severe decline for fifty years and offered token resistance to the invaders. The weakening of the region as a result of the drought laid the groundwork for the susceptibility to the plague of Europe.

Barbarians brought about the fall of classical civilization by sacking Rome in 476 A.D. Byzantine civilization in the eastern Mediterranean, however, collapsed about 100 years later after a bubonic plague swept the region and after invasions by Slavic tribes and Persians.

In addition to the drought, disease, and marauding; evidence also indicates that a global event contributed to the inception of the Dark Ages. In 536 A.D. a violent volcanic eruption occurred and filled the atmosphere with a thick layer of dust. The world fell into a darkness that was likened unto a solar eclipse and whose effects lasted for over a year.

A worldwide account of a massive climatic change, caused by a volcanic eruption in New Guinea in 536 A. D. created strange effects that were recorded by observers from Rome to China. There were those who noted that the sun went dark for more than a year, and all the crops failed. Procopius of Greece in 536 A.D writes:

> *The Sun gave forth its light without brightness, like the Moon, during this whole year, and it seemed very much like the Sun in eclipse, for the beams it shed were not clear*

Another source, the Roman writer Cassiodorus said:

> *We have had a winter without storms, spring without mildness, and summer without heat. Whence can we hope for mild weather, when the months that once ripened the crops have been deadly sick under the northern blasts? ...Out of all the elements, we find these two opposed to us: perpetual frost and unnatural drought."*

Evidence for this unnatural climatic period comes from tree-ring data in several parts of the world. Ancient trees such as the

4,000-year-old Bristle Cone pines in California show that the years around 540 A.D. were those of the least growth in four millennia.

Medical and natural disasters alone would certainly have crippled the infrastructure of a culture. And those occurrences alone would have had far reaching effects for future generations. History, however, does provide examples of tough times, coupled with strong leadership, and successful outcomes. Unfortunately, political expedience to maintain the approval of the populace is not a characteristic of strong leadership; and strong leadership might have lessened the effects of the Dark Ages.

Emperor Constantine I at the battle of the Milvian Bridge in 312 A. D. looked toward the sun and saw a vision of a cross. His interpretation of the revelation was; *by this, conquer.* The cross then became an insignia for the shields and flags of his army. It was an army that did not lose a battle thereafter.

It was customary at that time when entering Rome, victorious in battle, to offer sacrifices to the gods. Constantine broke tradition and bypassed the Capitoline, and went straight to the imperial palace without offering the usual thanks. This passive endorsement of Christianity, while not fully embracing its tenets, at least publically, was not an endorsement of paganism either. Constantine, however, did not at this time want to distance himself from the influential of Rome who was still practicing pagans.

In 313 A.D., Constantine announced toleration for Christianity in the Edict of Milan. Prior to the act, smaller accommodations had been made to permit religious liberty to practice one's faith. The Milan treatise removed all restrictions placing Christians on equal footing with pagan religions.

With the newfound freedom to openly worship as they pleased, Christian leaders took advantage of the political environment and promoted their monotheistic theology. Angered by a history of persecution, and intimidated by a society of intellectual liberalism, the Bishops, priests and parishioners sought by the means of persuasion and intimidation a final solution of their own.

Many examples exist that demonstrates the Christian church's paranoia. One was the burning of a library. The Royal Library of Alexandria was once the largest in the world. It is usually assumed to have been founded at the beginning of the $3^{rd}$ century B.C. during the reign of Ptolemy II of Egypt after his father had set up the temple of the Muses, the Musaeum, which is the origin of the word Museum. The initial organization is attributed to Demetrius Phalereus, and is estimated to have stored at its peak 400,000 to 700,000 parchment scrolls.

One story holds that the Library was seeded with Aristotle's own private collection, through one of his students, the same Demetrius Phalereus that founded the museum. Other collections were secured by decree of Ptolemy III of Egypt. All visitors to the city were required to surrender all books and scrolls in their possession; these writings were then swiftly copied by official scribes. The originals were put into the Library, and the copies were delivered to the previous owners. Although this practice encroached on the rights of the traveler or merchant, it was a necessary act to create a repository of books in the relatively new city.

One of the reasons so little is known about the library is that it was lost centuries after its creation. All that is left of many of the volumes are tantalizing titles that hint at all the history lost from the building's destruction. It is believed that 123 plays of Sophocles were stored in the library, only seven survived. One of those seven is *Oedipus Rex*. Similar numbers apply to the works of other authors. Eratosthenes, a contemporary of the library was a poet, philosopher, astronomer and chief librarian in the 3rd century B.C. He calculated the diameter of the Earth more than 15 centuries before Copernicus and Galileo. Aristarchus of Samos wrote about the heliocentric hypothesis, which stated that the Earth and the planets revolve around the Sun. Euclid wrote 13 books on mathematics, particularly geometry called *The Elements*, which provided a comprehensive analysis of geometry, proportions, and theory of numbers, and also had some notable studies in geometrical optics. Archimedes wrote about the up-thrust theory, and invented the pump known as Archimedes' screw which is still used today.

Medical schools were a part of the library and the most eminent professor was Herophilus of Chalcedon who chronicled the difference between sensory and motor nerves. Another school founded by Philinus thoroughly studied anatomy, physiology and experimental therapeutics. Later, the best of both schools were combined by Heracleides of Tarentum, who practiced human anatomy and developed surgical techniques, while maintaining the experimental method of cure. Alexandria's reputation in the study of medicine attracted Galen. He studied the muscles, spinal cord, heart, urinary system, and proved that the arteries are full of blood. Galen was the last of the great physicians of the ancient world. In the 4th century A.D., Marcellinus the eminent historian wrote:

> *Medicine continues to grow greater from day to day, so that a doctor who wishes to establish his standing in the profession can dispense with the need for any proof of it by saying that he was trained at Alexandria.*

One might say if the work of Hippocrates represents the foundation of the development of the practice of medicine; Galen's work represented the zenith.

The Museum housed the writings of famous poets and philosophers such as Philitas, the tutor of Ptolemy II, who was much concerned with the collection and interpretation of rare poetic words. His pupil Zenodotus of Ephesus wrote the first critical edition of Homer and other poets. The great poet Callimachus compiled the Pinakes which means Tablets. The Pinakes was a vast catalogue of the chief authors and national bibliography, which remained as a standard reference work of Greek literature until the Byzantine period. He also wrote a book opposing Praxiphanes the chief Peripatetic, which is one who promotes the teachings of Aristotle. Philosophy in Alexandria flourished. With the expansion of the Roman Empire, Alexandria bred its own philosophers; Theodorus the Atheist, Hegasias the Advocate of Suicide, and Antiochus of Ascalon. Religious philosophy also developed among the Jews and the Christians and was influenced by pagan philosophers.

Jealousy and rivalry developed between students of ancient Alexandria, and those of other schools throughout the classical world, particularly Athens. Synesius, Bishop of Cyrene wrote in a letter:

> *Athens has no longer anything sublime except the country's famous names. Today Egypt has received and cherishes the fruitful wisdom of Hypatia. Athens was aforetime the dwelling-place of the wise; today the bee-keepers alone bring it honor.*

Few events in ancient history are as controversial as the destruction of the Library, as the historical record is both contradictory, and incomplete. There are three accounts if its ruin. Not surprisingly, the Great Library became a symbol for knowledge itself, and its destruction was attributed to those who were portrayed as ignorant barbarians, often for purely political reasons.

The last Chief Librarian was a mathematician, astronomer, physicist and the head of the Neoplatonic School of Philosophy. These accomplishments were rare for anyone then, or now, and rarer still for woman. Her name is Hypatia. And her talents, skills and confidence that would at the very least be enviable if she were a man became a threat because of gender. She was often courted by suitors, and never accepted their offers. Hypatia was at the epicenter of many political influences. Cyril, the Arch Bishop of Alexandria loathed her. His parishioners murdered Hypatia as she commuted to work. The mob ripped the flesh from her bones with seashells, she succumbed to the attack and died in 415 A.D. – she was 45 years old. Her office and home were ransacked, and the contents destroyed. Later, the library was burned. The scrolls were used to heat the public baths of the city. Hypatia and the Library are distance memories, all but forgotten, and Cyril was made a Saint.

Some have said this event marked the beginning of 1,000 years of lost knowledge; only to have that knowledge rediscovered in the Age of Enlightenment. And even then, the practice of destroying the works of the so-called heathen in the New World was ordained and sanctioned by the Church.

Natural disasters that included famines and volcanoes, a pandemic that was spread by fleas on the backs of rats, and a political environment that endorsed a type of self-inflicted lobotomy that was an attempt to rid the world of paganism certainly contributed to the rise of the Dark Ages. These hardships, as horrible and destructive as they were, were not the most significant factors.

The people of the world had experienced natural disasters before this time. And disease and political oppression were certainly not a new occurrence. The timing of these combined events within a couple hundred years of each other culminating around 500 A.D. is noteworthy. But, where were those that were heralded as miracle workers of the ancient world? Where were the demigods that were chronicled in history and folklore? Where were the Caesars, the Avatars, the Christ, and the Buddha at a time when humanity needed them the most? All ears of the Western world were willing to hear and all minds willing to accept answers to the problems that plagued humankind.

## The Answer

*There was a certain woman that dwelt beyond Jordan, her name was Mary; her father was Eleazar, of the village Bethezob, which signifies the house of Hyssop. She was eminent for her family and her wealth, and had fled away to Jerusalem with the rest of the multitude, and was with them besieged therein at this time. The other effects of this woman had been already seized upon, such I mean as she had brought with her out of Perea, and removed to the city. What she had treasured up besides, as also what food she had contrived to save, had been also carried off by the rapacious guards, who came every day running into her house for that purpose. This put the poor woman into a very great passion, and by the frequent reproaches and imprecations she east (slanders) at these rapacious villains, she had provoked them to anger against her; but none of them, either out of the indignation she had raised against herself, or out of commiseration of her case, would take away her life; and if she found any food, she perceived her labors were for others, and not for herself; and it was now become impossible for her any way to find any more food, while the famine pierced through her very bowels and marrow, when also her passion was fired to a degree beyond the famine itself; nor did she consult with anything but with her passion and the necessity she was in. She then attempted a most unnatural thing; and snatching up her son, who was a child sucking at her breast, she said, "O thou miserable infant! For whom shall I preserve thee in this war, this famine, and this sedition? As to the war with the Romans, if they preserve our lives, we must be slaves. This famine also will destroy us, even before that slavery comes upon us. Yet are these seditious rogues more terrible than both the other. Come on; be thou my food, and be thou a fury to these seditious varlets, and a by-word to the world, which is all that is now wanting to complete the calamities of us Jews." As soon as she had said this, she slew her son, and then roasted him, and eats the one half of him, and kept the other half by her concealed. Upon this the seditious came in presently, and smelling the horrid scent of this food, they threatened her that they would cut her throat immediately if she did not show them what food she had gotten ready. She replied that she had saved a very fine portion of it for them, and withal uncovered what was left of her son. Hereupon they were seized with a horror and amazement of mind, and stood astonished at the sight, when she said to them, "This is mine own son, and what hath been done was mine own doing! Come; eat of this food; for I have eaten of it myself! Do not you pretend to be either more tender than a woman, or more compassionate than a mother; but if you be so scrupulous, and do abominate this my sacrifice, as I have eaten the one half, let the rest be reserved for me also." After which those men went out trembling, being never so much affrighted at anything as they were at this, and with some difficulty they left the rest of that meat to the mother. Upon which the whole city was full of this horrid action immediately; and while everybody laid this miserable case before their own eyes, they trembled, as if this unheard of action had been done by themselves. So those that were thus distressed by the famine were very desirous to die, and those already dead were esteemed happy, because they had not lived long enough either to hear or to see such miseries.*

Jerusalem was a besieged city. Jewish factions engaged in civil war, and the unrest had affected all aspects of life. The preceding example chronicled by Flavius Josephus illustrates the conditions inside the walled city. Famine and crime were common place, and unspeakable acts sickened even the most hardened. To save the city and preserve human life, the Romans under the leadership of Titus encircled Jerusalem. Roman law required preserving local customs as in the case of religious freedom. Roman law would not, however, permit civil uprising and Titus made attempts to negotiate a settlement between the warring factions with no success. This necessitated military intervention. The city was destroyed; the stone Temple burned and flowed like molten rock through the streets of the Holy City. And what happened next is documented by two credible historians.

A battle occurred in the skies above Jerusalem in 70 A.D. Josephus and Tacitus recorded the events that took place. Flavius Josephus writes:

> *I suppose the account of it would seem to be a fable, were it not related by those that saw it, and were not the events that followed it of so considerable a nature as to deserve such signals; for, before sunsetting, chariots and troops of soldiers in their armor were seen running about among the clouds, and surrounding of cities. Moreover, at that feast which we call Pentecost, as the priests were going by night into the inner [court of the temple,] as their custom was, to perform their sacred ministrations, they said that, in the first place, they felt a quaking, and heard a great noise, and after that they heard a sound as of a great multitude, saying, "Let us remove hence."*

Tacitus was an equally prestigious Roman historian writes:

> *Prodigies had occurred, which this nation, prone to superstition, but hating all religious rites, did not deem it lawful to expiate by offering and sacrifice. There had been seen hosts joining battle in the skies, the fiery gleam of arms, the temple illuminated by a sudden radiance from the clouds. The doors of the inner shrine were suddenly thrown open, and a voice*

*of more than mortal tone was heard to cry that the*
*gods were departing. At the same instant there was a*
*mighty stir as of departure.*

The battle of the gods in the skies, and their subsequent departure marked the beginning of the decline of the Classical world. The departure of those that were the descendents of the Nephilim and the Sons of God was the beginning of the end of extreme mentoring that had created the gifted leaders of Egypt, Greece and Rome; and Asia and the Americas. Their absence, and the subsequent dying-off of the super-humans that were groomed as managers of the rank and file, slowly eroded the knowledge and skills base that affected all aspects of life for centuries to come.

The art, science and economy that had served Europe and the surrounding regions so well withered as an autumn leaf. The economy floundered as a result of the pandemic. Science knowledge was lost due to the newly acquired political control of the Church and its paranoia of pagan influences. The arts suffered as a result of both economic pressures and political posturing. All in all, without the leadership, oppressive, or not, of these departed demigods, life was without a path to follow, and the life of the Classical world lost its way. Compromise and surrender to abject mysticism was the rule of the day.

Lacking the understanding of physical and medical science, the Middle Agers were fearful of what tomorrow held in store for them. Without access to historical records to piece together humanity's collective experience, every happening was new and wrought with anxiety. Superstition fueled by the most basic of human fears – darkness, whether real or symbolic, created prejudice against minorities and cast blame on the innocent factions of society.

# THE SPLIT

*Science without religion is lame, religion without science is blind.*
Albert Einstein

The Dark, or Middle Ages lasted for a thousand years. Beginning in approximately 500 AD and ending about 1500 AD, humanity wandered about without direction and wondered about existing, with basic subsistence the top priority. In 1095 a desperate message was received by Pope Urban II from the Byzantine Emperor, Comnenus. The message was a plea for the Pope to send forces to stave off the armies of Muslim Turks. On November 27, the Pope addressed an assembly of soldiers gathered at Clermont, France and with a rallying cry, *God Wills It,* the first Crusade was launched. The first was considered the most successful of the eight and with each the spoils of war were plundered. Pillaging the Holy Land of its relics and hidden secrets from the time of the Demigods, the returning armies supplied Europe with an ever increasing knowledge base. Then slowly what had been lost of the Classical world was rediscovered, and with that knowledge a new set of problems; responsibility for managing power that knowledge affords. The sleeping giant slowly awakened to a new world order.

A number of enlightened individuals are credited with discoveries. And each discovery represents a candle's flame to illuminate the intellectual darkness. These discoveries did not come without the reward of accusations of heresy, however. The church's fear of pagan influences and the lack of confidence and resolve of the masses to mandate tolerance created an environment of oppression and superstition. Under the guise of holiness and spiritualism, superstition and prejudice made the pangs of change extreme.

Change did occur and there were certain members of the populace that rediscovered the works of antiquity. Enthusiasm for art, literature and lifestyle of classical Greece and Rome made the rounds in certain social circles. And the evolution of a new subculture that placed an emphasis on the abilities and skills of humankind while discounting the spiritual tenets of the church gained popularity.

For this new subculture to be successful relative to the status the church held in one's daily life, it had to have its own theology and set of clergy. Secular Humanism was the belief system and the scientist, the enlightened individuals that are credited with discovering or developing what was previously known and developed by the ancients, were the clergy. This group, much like the church, had its own set of rituals and customs.

The golden rule of this new religion was, *hypothesize, test and observe*. And any axiom that could not be supported by this golden rule was to be discarded as untenable and useless. As if the available resources to support the standards of the golden rule were without reproach and limits.

The humanist began to legitimize their belief system by discrediting selected church doctrines. In 1537 Andreas Vesalius, a Belgian physician, published *De Fabrica Corpis Humani* that documented that men did not have fewer ribs than women thus discrediting the creation story of Genesis. Similar attacks on the church were numerous. The most profound being that of Nicholas Copernicus and his publication, *De Revolutionibus Orbium Caelestium*. It was a writing that promoted the heliocentric – sun centered – solar system, an idea that placed earth in an inferior position in the cosmos and minimized man's importance in creation.

Certainly these discoveries have immeasurable value in the awakening of the mind of the Western world, and most were factual and appropriate. And there were apologists that attempted to keep one foot in faith and the other in science, but these were rare occurrences and were not the prime directive of the new movement, a movement whose passion quickly gained strength.

Over time this new movement of Secular Humanism experienced growing pangs as well. Polarization of ideas created two philosophical camps. One group migrated to Paris and promoted an atheistic tome and the other to Berlin and supported an agnostic perspective. Atheism, an absence of belief in deities and, agnosticism, an assertion that there is no way to know one way or the other, defined what would ultimately lead to one of the greatest tragedies of human history.

Voltaire, Hume and Rousseau were the Empiricists. And their headquarters in Paris was a fertile setting for their extreme ideas. Paris was still heavily influenced by the Catholic Church, and this equal but opposite reaction to its tenets created extremes in philosophical arguments. The Empiricists' foundation was anchored in the belief that nature is governed by a set of natural laws that can be observed and measured; and this measuring and observing results in unambiguous, *empirical* data that cannot be refuted.

At the same time, Kant, Fichte, Schelling and Schlegel were developing their own perspective in Berlin. Unfettered by religious constraints, Martin Luther had already led Germany into Reformation; this gave this set of philosophers more freedom. Accepting the Empiricists' perspective that natural laws exists, and that there are observable and measurable aspects of our existence, they also held to an idea that this method did not provide an avenue to explain why humans exist.

Hegel believed that human intelligence evolved from generation to generation. And he also promoted the tenet that there exist a universal spirit that shaped history and moves man to a higher level of social consciousness. The two groups from the Catholic Church's perspective were, nonetheless, two peas in a pod. Comparing and contrasting the two, however, would uncover fundamental differences that would soon become apparent.

The Church's stronghold on society was unquestioned from the fall of the Classical Age to the eighteenth century. The rise of Secular Humanism and its attacks on the beliefs and principles of the church took its toll. For some it pushed them closer to their faith, and for others it was a defining moment of apostasy. So the division between those who held Judaism, Christianity and Islam in high esteem and those that adopted the Humanists *belief* widened. And this ever widening chasm often pushed members of either side to believe in more extreme or activist concepts; and one of the most radical was Darwin's theory of evolution.

A contemporary of Darwin was James Hutton. He published a treatise that suggested the world is much older than originally thought. Another contemporary of Darwin, Jean Baptiste Lamarck, published a writing classifying species on a *ladder of nature* ranking them from the simplest to the most complex. In addition to the ladder analogy, Lamarck insisted that characteristics of a species would be inherited – passed on – to succeeding generations. The concepts of Hutton, Lamarck, and others captured Darwin's imagination. Motivated by a general prejudice to discredit religious dogma, and by an intriguing hypothesis based on the concept of an extremely old earth and a ladder of increasing biological complexity, Darwin published The Origin of Species in 1859.

The Empiricists embraced Darwin's theory as the final death knell for the church's creation story. Discounting recorded history and eye witness accounts chronicled by the ancients as myth, they were by sheer magnitude of time able to eclipse the few thousand years of recorded history with billions of years of geological and paleontological *evidence*. This, in their minds, eliminated all intellectual competition.

The Empiricists promoted their dominate theory with the promise of producing the missing link between primates and man. In fulfillment of the prediction made by the Berlin agnostics, the branch of Secular Humanist in Paris had become a cult – a religion of their own. And, perhaps, its most famous practitioner was an infamous dictator.

Darwin proposed that natural and artificial selection would affect the evolution of a species. Natural selection as random mutation and artificial selection by intervention of a third party as a catalyst for change. And it was this simple concept that influenced Adolf Hitler to incorporate Social Darwinism into his final solution. Hitler saw the intermarrying of the German people with foreigners as an incipient threat to the Aryan bloodline, and ultimately to national security. And his remedy would be a third party intervention in the form of artificial selection.

His plan was threefold. First, there was to be a prohibition of marrying anyone of the savage races. Second, eliminate the defects that would jeopardize the gene pool. The defects were defined as gays, the mentally and physically retarded, criminals – anyone that was not politically expedient. And third was to eliminate the unwanted races within German borders.

Darwin's dogma alleviated the moral obligation for doctors and scientists to treat people as human beings. Relegating individuals to groups that either adversely affect cultural and biological evolution, or who are adversely affected by it, allowed policy makers to do what they wished with large segments of the population. And in doing what they wished to have no feelings of remorse or pity, as these emotions could be defined as a defective character trait of the weak-minded. Justification for this type of treatment can be found in Darwin's Descent of Man:

> *With savages, the weak in body or mind are soon eliminated; and those that survive commonly exhibit a vigorous state of health. We civilised men, on the other hand, do our utmost to check the process of elimination; we build asylums for the imbecile, the maimed, and the sick; we institute poor-laws; and our medical men exert their utmost skill to save the life of every one to the last moment. There is reason to believe that vaccination has preserved thousands, who from a weak constitution would formerly have succumbed to small-pox. Thus the weak members of civilised societies propagate their kind. No one who has attended to the breeding of domestic animals will doubt that this must be highly injurious to the race of man. It is surprising how soon a want of care, or care wrongly directed, leads to the degeneration of a domestic race; but excepting in the case of man himself, hardly any one is so ignorant as to allow his worst animals to breed.*

Darwin continues suggesting a proactive approach to managing the herd and the suggestion did not fall on deaf ears. The Nazi regime followed the orders of their high priest to the utmost detail.

*The aid which we feel impelled to give to the helpless is mainly an incidental result of the instinct of sympathy, which was originally acquired as part of the social instincts, but subsequently rendered, in the manner previously indicated, more tender and more widely diffused. Nor could we check our sympathy, even at the urging of hard reason, without deterioration in the noblest part of our nature. The surgeon may harden himself whilst performing an operation, for he knows that he is acting for the good of his patient; but if we were intentionally to neglect the weak and helpless, it could only be for a contingent benefit, with an overwhelming present evil.*

History has characterized Hitler as a mad man that enjoyed killing. This is not entirely true. He is by definition a mass murderer, and is certainly wanton in his actions. There are no adequate apologizes to forgive him of his crimes. And some may tag him as mentally ill. He is arguably the criminal of the millennia. His motivation, however, stemmed from a desire to be a futuristic leader in preserving the Fatherland. And as a result, rationalization ruled as others were forced to make the ultimate accommodation.

His interpretation of the history of Rome and Greece led him to believe the fall of each was a result of internal factions and confusion. Confusion in that there was not a clear delineation of what a Greek or Roman was with respect to race and bloodline. And internal factions were defined as those individuals that did not have a clear nationalistic mission statement. And the inspiration to authorize and commit these heinous acts came from an author of a text that referred to people unlike him as savages. And the author whose inspiration came from his contemporaries and whose motivation came from an atheistic group of philosophers in Paris. And this group of philosopher's whose sole motivation was to destroy the influence of the Catholic Church. And this group of Philosophers' existence stemmed from a movement of secular humanists that attempted to find their way independent of the demigods that left the planet some 1,000 years earlier. Armed with a clear mission and endorsed by science, Hitler slaughtered fourteen million people with Darwin's blessing.

The effects of Darwinism exist to this day. The divorce of science and religion has created many modern day anomalies. Two examples are common topics of discussion. Extremes from the religious community that suggest that sexual intercourse is to be limited to procreation has had adverse effects on individuals and couples struggling to do the right thing. And the vilifying of contraception and masturbation as a sin against God has had similar results. All in all, the church throughout history has been suspect in its interpretation of healthy sex. The abstinence from sex for selected individuals within the church hierarchy so that they may retain a certain level of holiness suggests that those who have sex engage in acts that are less than divine. And far too often those that have taken this vow of chastity break their oath in a most tragic way further widening the chasm of credibility and dishonesty.

Science, on the other hand, has gone equally to the opposite extreme. Sexual promiscuity is condoned and even encouraged by

Western social morays, and often results in unwanted pregnancies. Western medical clinics that receive federal funding are mandated to provide confidential services to under aged patients. Services that compromise the parent / child relationship with secrets and pseudo morality, all the while, supporting the presumption the child knows best.

With Darwin's influence, medical science has defined an unborn fetus as a nonhuman. As an entity that is unviable and thus disposable. And one is likely to hear prominent politicians refer to unwanted children as mistakes that could have been avoided with a simple procedure. And this group of human-want-to-bes that are classified as less than human permits those that engineer the *corrective* procedures to perform these acts without feelings of pity or remorse. This echoes historical rationalizations from the holocaust.

In the beginning, when abortions were first made available, they were limited to extremes in medical scenarios; rape, incest or the existence of conditions that were detrimental to the mother's health. Today they are promoted as a right of an individual to make decisions regarding one's body. And if someone opposes that decision on moral or ethical grounds, they are characterized as religious fundamentalist, or as rightwing political extremists, or an enemy of one's right to choose what's best for their body. Thus, the rationalization to perform an abortion because the timing to have a baby is not right, or the gender is not preferred, or contraception was not available, or the baby deserves a stay-at-home father, is a continuation of Darwin's commandments regarding Artificial Selection.

Western culture forces one to either align themselves with religious dogma similar to the Catholic Church of the Middle Ages, or to side with science and become as the Empiricist of

Paris. The former defined as overly emotional and mystical and the later accepting only that which can be seen and measured. It is extremely difficult for some to visualize an existence where both the church and science can coexist. No one is conditioned for this to happen. And answers to a selected question would produce two distinct answers from either perspective. Compromise is akin to concession, and a stance in the middle angers proponents of either side of the dispute. And this alienation leaves one isolated and limited with regard to both support groups. And seemingly, that is a much too high a price for one to pay. Some simply lack the courage to take an independent stance.

The magnitude of these tidal forces and the effects it has on whom and what one becomes is great. The pressure to follow the path of least resistance to maintain a peer group's acceptance and to feel self actualized becomes foremost in one's thinking. Meandering through a floodplain of opportunities to grow, all the while ignoring or dodging opportunities to become enlightened; all of this to remain what others expect. It is unmistakably a contrast of one thinking deeply to one thinking clearly. And, certainly, clarity is much needed and rarely achieved.

Having the time and space to drill down through each layering of human experience, one would find themselves at the door of Western ideology. Where the struggle of the Middle Ages still exists. This struggle is defined as the temporal approach to the pursuit of the visible and measurable. As opposed to the spiritual approach to that which is sensed and imperceptible. The Following-the-Rules approach to mandating behavior suggests a formula that can be calculated and measured, or the Living-the-Rules based behavior that suggests an existence from a Higher Calling.

There is a spiritual aspect to nature as there is a physical. The two cannot be in opposition as the church, the hardcore humanists and scientist suggests. The apparent hostility displayed by both camps is a manifestation of frustration and fear; frustration in the elusive search for the Mind of God, and fear the other may find it first. Science, in its search for a unified theory of everything, and the religionists desire to have all things connected to a single source, appear to be on a different set of tracks. How do their approaches differ? They don't. The spectators are viewing the spiritual and physical world from different perspectives; watching the same events unfold from different seats in the theater while alternating their interpretations between style and substance. We all desire the same thing, to know our origins, to know why we are here, and to know our future: and to know how the three are connected.

Understanding on a macro level how Western thought has developed and how it influences one's thinking, it becomes clear to see why solutions are often heavily weighted toward a *show me* mentality. Emphasis on reporting without consideration of the source, point-and-click solutions that minimize human intervention and decisions made from a posturing of fear instead of love frames the picture of existence that guarantees want instead of abundance. And want in one's life usually manifest itself as unbridled competition to gain at any cost one's desires.

This win-at-all-cost mentality can be traced to another tragic event involving Charles Darwin. Darwin was a medical school dropout, and being from a wealthy family he was expected to be educated and respected. He chose to pursue a degree in divinity to fulfill the need of the former and greed to fulfill the need of the later. Volunteering to sail on the HMS Beagle, Darwin spent five years of his life traveling the globe. Chronicling his experiences and with a heart-felt disdain for the specialty of his degree, he wrote, *supposedly*, the <u>Origin of Species</u>.

Darwin had a contemporary that lived and studied biology in New Guinea. Alfred Russell Wallace was a member of the lower class of Europe. Self-taught and motivated, he made an income poaching animals to sell to zoos, curators and collectors. He was also very clever. He wrote a document similar to the conclusions in Darwin's famous book. The interesting caveat is that Wallace's writing predates Darwin's.

Wallace sent his manuscript to Darwin to ask for a peer review, and if acceptable, to forward it to Darwin's colleague, James Hutton – the geologist. Hutton was a close friend of Darwin and they collaborated to use Wallace's writing as their own. Darwin's comment to Hutton in letters exchanged between the two was that he could never let Wallace take credit for this idea. So, he used that document to create <u>Origin of Species</u>. Darwin is celebrated by many and Wallace remains a commoner. What is not generally known is the effect this piracy had on Western thought.

Darwin being from the upper class had a mentality of superiority. And Wallace being from the lower ranks had a realization of humility. Wallace's observations of nature was not one of survival of the fittest, it was a perspective of the non-survival of the weakest. The former suggest loftiness in one's position in life. And the latter inferred one's likelihood of becoming a member of the weakest. The former pronounced one's influence in controlling the weak - artificial selection. And the latter defined the realization that cooperation is foremost in survival. The theft of an idea and the plagiarism of a trusted document created an outlier that has created a world of competition instead of one of cooperation.

Explaining this to a parent of a little league baseball player is fruitless. Winning at all costs has become, not only a means to an end, it has become what most consider to be a gifted trait. And this sense of competition is not isolated to the playing field; it affects every aspect of life. Bernie Madoff, Ken Lay, Richard Scrushy and a seemingly endless list of unscrupulous politicians and profiteers have defined to what end the *survival of fittest* will go to maintain competitiveness.

So it is not difficult to see that the blending of science and religion will not automatically produce a hybrid way of thinking that will lead to change. The two are competitive and are fallen aspects of a higher existence. Can it change? Can what has been done be reversed? To change culture is to change our thinking – the source of our beliefs - and to do that is to fully experience the emotion of a single word; a word that moves the Mind of God.

# THE HEARTBEAT OF THE DIVINE

*You ask: what is the meaning or purpose of life?*
*I can only answer with another question:*
*Do you think we are wise enough to read God's mind?*
Freeman Dyson

We are spiritual beings with a great curiosity about nature. And that curiosity demands more than just an answer to a question, it craves an understanding. And when one seeks understanding from a singular perspective, from either the scientific or the religious standpoints, the answer is less than whole. In fact, the incomplete answer is more frustrating than no answer at all. The possibility for all-inclusive answers to questions and to feel whole in one's comprehension leads to a boldness to step out and reexamine one's beliefs.

This reexamining of beliefs is a consciousness that proposed answers from a singular perspective are lacking and suspect; and that collaborative solutions from both perspectives are often mere negotiations and compromise. The courage of one's questions and the depth of one's answers lie beyond the unification of science and religion. And the source of fearlessness is in the reexamining of beliefs that each person is both the answer and the understanding; as if each individual is a part of that which one seeks.

The blending of the desire to experience physically that which we call nature and the need to transcend that same desire to connect to the Source is the seed of Spirituality that exist in all of us. We are God's greatest thought. We are, in fact, God thinking. We are both a part of that which is created and that which creates. And when one fully understands that relationship the realization becomes clear that what we think affects the things around us. In fact, it creates what we expect to experience; the Mind of God.

Max Karl Ernst Ludwig Planck was one of the most important German physicists of the late 19th and early 20th century, winning the Nobel Prize in Physics in 1918. He is considered to be the inventor of quantum theory. His insight to the nature of the Mind of God is revealed in a speech delivered in Florence, Italy in 1944,

> *"As a man who has devoted his whole life to the most clear-headed science, to the study of matter, I can tell you as a result of my research about atoms this much: There is no matter as such. All matter originates and exists only by virtue of a force which brings the particle of an atom to vibration and holds this most minute solar system of the atom together. We must assume behind this force the existence of a conscious and intelligent mind. This mind is the matrix of all matter."*

All matter originates and exists only by virtue of a force. Our primordial intuition whispers to us of our intimate connection to nature. Science enlightens us to a great release of energy and matter at the Big Bang. Creation stories speak to us of a consciousness that willed into existence the very universe that captures our imagination. And it is this connection, through the very atoms that comprises all matter, that we know the Mind of God. To know the Mind of God is to know ourselves. We are the very reason this connection exists.

Western science has confirmed ancient traditions that an intelligent field of energy exist that bathes all of creation. And this field of energy serves as a vessel for all that is, or has been, or will ever be. It also provides a gateway for inner emotions of humanness to integrate with creation itself. And more remarkably, it functions as a mirror to re-create our most heartfelt intent in physical reality. One's expectation creates creation. And as human experience pushes the boundaries of the heavens and the limits of the quantum world, as we peer further into space and deeper into the microscopic realm, matter is created because we expect it to be where we look. All matter originates from this field as disturbances – wrinkles and folds – in the fabric of the matrix. And our thoughts – emotions – affect these disturbances.

Experiments were conducted in 1881 by Michelson and Morley to measure the energy of the matrix. Their claim to fame is conducting the *Best Failed Experiment*. Their attempt to test the ether wind, the energy of the matrix, failed to produce any results. It is as if Michelson or Morley moistened an index finger and extended it upward on a still day and concluded that wind does not exist. The absence of a measurable outcome meant there was nothing to measure. And what they failed to recognize is that they were a part of the energy they were attempting to measure. Planck said it best,

> *"Science cannot solve the ultimate mystery of*
> *nature. And that is because, in the last analysis,*

*we ourselves are a part of the mystery that we are
trying to solve."*

So, it can be said that one may not feel the wind if one is moving
with the wind.

Two schools of thought at the time were fundamentally
different in many ways. One concept held by Einstein and others
is that the universe exists and we as humans have no effect on
it, one way or another, an approach that seems similar to the
Empiricist's of Paris perspective of God. And the second concept
is that consciousness creates matter. And that's why the universe
at the grandest, or the minutest scale, seems to promote the divine,
a cosmos without end.

Research is leading to a conclusion that humans are not an
incidental aspect of creation, existing as a result of happenstance.
And we are not subjected to a capricious set of rules that makes each
waking moment a fearful experience. We are instead responsible
for an ongoing creation as conscious entities existing in a universe
of consciousness; we are a way for creation to know itself – in fact
the two are inseparable, both one in the same. Neville, a visionary
from the island of Barbados, stated that,

> *Man's chief delusion is his conviction that there are
> other causes (in creation) other than his own state
> of consciousness.*

Humans possess all the abilities that are needed to create all of the
things that are wanted. And the abilities hinge on how our attitude
affects our consciousness.

Pythagoras and Aristotle described what they called the fifth
element to earth, wind, fire and water as *ether*. This is an element

that fills a supposed void that some scientist believe exists between particles and planets. Experts have suggested that well over ninety nine percent of creation is empty. And if the empty space was filled by its constituent elements – compressed to fill the void – it could be reduced to the size of a green pea. Physicist Konrad Finagle stated that,

> *Space is what keeps everything from happening in the same place.*

And that in its self suggests that the emptiness of space, both the microscopic and macroscopic, is anything but empty.

If space is empty, how can waves of light or sound pass through its void? It is as if we expect waves to crash onto the shore without the existence of water. The energy of the wave in the ocean requires a mode of transportation as does the waves of light or sound through space. And the ocean of emptiness that permits the waves of light from distant galaxies to reach the eyes of the curious, or the sound of pulsars to reach the ears of the inquisitive is the energy of the matrix. The ether of the ancients has become the wind of the contemporary as we pass through its effects.

In 1986 E. W. Silvertooth conducted the same experiment that Michelson and Morley had attempted, but with equipment that was much more sensitive. Sponsored by the Air Force, he detected the *ether wind* that had eluded Michelson and Morley. And the data supports the existence of ambient energy in nature that produces characteristic effects as objects pass through it, as the wind on one's face while jogging in the park. And it is the existence of this matter that permits the transference of light and sound as waves through what was once thought to be the void of space. The same *ether* that fills the void between the galaxies occupies the space between atoms.

Ancient Vedic literature describes these infinitely small particles as *Bhuttatmas*. And in the Vedic expressions of Creation, these are the first material forms which come into existence from the realm of Pure Spirit. In the Vedic literature, these infinitely small particles have *awareness*, and are considered the smallest units of Consciousness, as well as the smallest units of matter. The *Aether*, the Mind of God, is composed of various combinations of *Bhuttatmas*, comprising sub-quantum particles, as well as unfettered *Bhuttatmas*. According to the Vedic text, the electron is composed of literally trillions of these tiny bits of consciousness.

These sub-quantum conscious particles act as an operating system for creation, with the ability to provide a platform on which the software of human intent is processed. Human emotion – the power of feeling – is the program that wrinkles and folds the matrix to reflect what we project onto it; that is to create matter and reality. Reality is created with heartfelt emotion and intent.

Prayers of supplication which originate from greed or vanity are ineffectual. Desire for something pushes it away because the desire itself becomes the answered prayer of supplication; because it is based solely on ego. And the difference in the two is a matter of perspective; seeing yourself from the result or seeing yourself working toward it. The latter prompts within one a need for instruction and guidance the former a deep sense of gratitude. And Gratitude moves the Mind of God.

The matrix, the Mind of God, mirrors human emotion and no emotion has more effect than gratitude. So, if one *wishes* a certain outcome then one must be genuinely grateful for that reality. This is much more difficult that simply praying for a desired result, it is the essence of faith and the acceptance of what is. And faith is more how we see our role in the matrix as it is any rehearsed dogma.

The manifestation of this faith begins with the acceptance of things in our belief system that supposedly do not make sense. This acceptance is the belief in our potential and not our limitations. In the original text of the Gnostic Gospels, Christ's statement, "Whatsoever you ask the Father in my name, He will give it to you..." had the added text of; *so ask without hidden motive and be surrounded by your answer...* This suggests that prayer – ask and you will receive – is more a state of being than an intermittent action. One should be surrounded by the answer – living in a state of acceptance. And that there are limitations in what one could ask and expect results; limitations are based on ego – so ask without hidden motive.

One cannot opt out of the matrix. One cannot, not be a part of the Mind of God. To exist is to be in the matrix and we as conscious beings eternally exist. And to be in the matrix is to function within its framework. The matrix is a vessel for all that exists. We are creating *things* in this field of energy, knowingly, or not. And human emotion is the catalyst for change within this framework. Western thought has vilified the experience and expression of emotion as a characteristic of the weak or the uneducated. And this philosophy has focused our attention on what we don't want in life, the bad outcomes. Thus we focus our attention on the external world around us.

An industry of fear based on the need for medical and life insurance, security systems, retirement funding, and a laundry listing of things *responsible* individuals plan for in anticipating the worst, has become a lucrative business. This expenditure of energy and worry on what may happen instead of focusing on the world within us has created a tragic disconnect from what we once were to what we have now become. This conditioning has softened our senses and hardened our hearts to a primeval aspect of our inner being, to simply accept the things we want. And *want* is defined as that which we need as opposed to that which we wish to acquire.

The maturity that comes with this understanding filters from our consciousness greed and vengeance as unthinkable acts. So, the power of the Matrix is not an Aladdin's Lamp of wishes to be used to cause harm to others or to expand one's holdings at the expense of others. Desires based upon ego are not emotions that are based on compassion. And compassion is a type of Gratitude that is extended to others. It too is a feeling that moves the Matrix. Compassion is achieved when there is no judgment regarding the rightness or wrongness of an outcome, or simply stated, one's ego is not effected one way or another. The misguidance of this focus prompts the question as to how much effort is wasted on diversions in one's life instead of on orchestrations; how often one views themselves as a victim as opposed to being a participant.

The matrix is also a bridge, or an avenue to navigate within its confines, and its confines are limited only by human observation. And this permits the capacity for telepathy, remote viewing, intuition, and physic abilities; as well as other experiences Western civilization tags as mystical, or daunting. Time and space do not exist in the Mind of God. And experiments have demonstrated that at the quantum level what is done at the present to a subatomic particle changes its characteristics in the past; as if time is stuck in a perpetual *now*.

Other experiments have also demonstrated that entangled particles that are separated by extreme distances are affected instantaneously when one is modified; as if distance and nature's speed limit of 186,000 miles per second does not apply. And stranger still, experiments that place human DNA in closed containers with photons have demonstrated life's ability to permanently change the characteristics of matter – in effect, create matter. The presence of life at any level of existence affects the matrix. And the energy that connects matter is also a part of that which it connects, matter.

The great apostasy in science is to suggest that the Laws of Physics are not universal. At the quantum level matter acts *spooky* and energy can be either a particle or a wave or both. These characteristics can happen at the same time, and it is the consciousness of the observer as to how energy behaves that opens the door of potential. In fact, the mathematics of the quantum world does not equate the actual existence of particles, or where they are, or how they will react; the mathematics provides a listing of potential characteristics and possible positions and the observer chooses a single solution.

The phenomenon of instantaneous reactions and the marvel of modifying the past suggest the whole of creation is represented in the very small. And that the whole of creation exist in a time called *now*. Hologram is a word created from a Greek term *holos* and *gramma* which means the whole picture. And the smallest piece of a hologram contains a complete representation – a whole picture – of the entire image. Modifying one aspect of hologram changes all representative images; both small and large. And the matrix may be best described as a hologram of existence as we know it. What is done at the local level by human intent then suggests that all of creation mirrors that change. So, change at any level does not have to travel any distance to change the whole because it is one.

An account chronicled by the Spanish when exploring the New World provides an example of a holographic universe. Spanish ships made anchor off the South American coast. Making their way to shore using smaller boats, the team of explorers was met by a shaman – a medicine man from a local village. The shaman obviously saw the explorers and the small boats at the shoreline, but could not see the ships anchored off shore even though the vessels were within eyesight. The explorers described the wooden vessel and the framework of sails and riggings, yet without previous experience and exposure to this type of craft the shaman saw nothing. Straining to detect telltale signs, the shaman first saw ripples as the ship displaced the water around it. Then looking from the corner of his eye a fuzzy image became visible and then a clear panorama of the ship was seen.

The villagers were unable to see the ship until the shaman had *learned* to see the vessel. And it was at that time, as if the ability to see was passed to each, the villagers saw the remarkable ship and its sails and riggings. The shaman paved the way and affected the holographic universe at the local level – his level – and that change affected the *whole picture* of the village. The ability to make a change, changes everything.

The question then arises why we as a species suffer from disease and misfortune. Why does the planet experience undue stress as a result of human interaction? Why do loved ones have to die? And why are we a threat to ourselves? Einstein was credited with the statement that we can't solve a problem while we are in the same level of thinking that created it. The answer then lies within the paradigm of what role we see ourselves in the matrix.

Are we characters that inadvertently affect the matrix? Are we subjected to uncontrollable edicts of the matrix? Evidence shows that we are conscious, active members of the matrix. And that we are entities that are in and a part of the field of energy that serves as a vessel for creation. And that we are a part of an avenue for navigating within it. And that we project an image – human intent – onto the mirror of the matrix that creates reality!

There is a fundamental, yet subtle difference in making a choice and then taking actions on that choice. This difference is best visualized as seeing oneself having arrived at a destination or still in route to that destination. Unless there are new thoughts and feelings that are the result of choice, reality may not change. And it is at that time disappointment and unproductive emotions take the place of prayer. And it is the substituting of prayer with these negative emotions – which is our interface to the Divine – that causes human grief.

Just as those who chant and utilize gongs and chimes as a part of a prayer ritual, these same chants, gongs and chimes are not the actual prayers. It is the feelings – the emotions – these activities create within the chanter that are the prayers. And it is within this framework of the Divine that one can have a prayerful moment in the viewing of a sunset, or in the sound of the crashing of the waves at the shoreline, or in the contemplation of one's place in creation, or in remembrance of a sacrifice made by a redeemer. Prayer is what moves us to experience genuine, heartfelt emotion. And prayer transports our minds to a place where miracles can become reality. And to occupy the place where emotion and reality meet is to feel the heartbeat of the Divine and to know the Mind of God.

# WAVES OF POSSIBILITIES

*We have more possibilities available in*
*each moment than we realize.*
Thich Nhat Hanh

The ritual of work, and the daily pilgrimage from home to the office on Westheimer Street was supposed to be the therapy to liberate myself from depression. At this point in my life, I was still wrestling with guilt and anger and the need to exact some form of vengeance on those that caused my Mother's death. And I tried to play the part of normalcy and act as though nothing had happened. Meet and greet as if yesterday had been long forgotten and that the promise of tomorrow is just a whimsical fantasy. In other words, get over it and focus on the tasks at hand. Neither of those philosophies, however, provided motivation or consolation. My coping mechanism was self destructive in many ways.

The most hurtful acts were the exclusion of family and friends from my life. Those acts were an attempt to distance myself from the pain and the blame. And this contradiction of the exclusion of loved ones, and the need to retain bitter memories of the past, did not make sense. It was as if I were holding on to the past with one hand, and pushing away the present with the other. And added to that, my hope of a better tomorrow was further compounded by my confusion, rendering me at times disheartened in my resolve. My emotions were scattered about as so many leaves in a park and the concept of *now* never entered my mind. And there is never a time when *now* does not exist and it was there I would find my deliverance.

The therapy that was most effective came in the form of intervention, and it was the persistent encouragement of friends who attempted to focus my attention on the *now*. Recognizing my self-imposed exile from reality, my interventionalist attempted a number of incentives to jolt my awareness toward pleasant memories of the past. And the first course of therapy of my healing came in the form of an insistent invitation; an evening out, a glass of wine and dinner at Mark's. To decline this invitation would have been madness. This bistro had been designated as one of Houston's best. The golden ceiling of this 1920's renovated church reflects ambient light onto the hand painted deco walls. And the added luminance of the candle lit tables creates cozy settings for private gatherings. Intimacy and atmosphere hold equal footing with culinary delights. Every aspect of this experience heightened all of one's senses; a corporeal pleasure. And the experience would certainly take my mind off the demons that tormented me.

The first course was a Jonah filled zucchini blossom, Texas crab cake and a Crisfield Maryland soft shell crab with avocado salsa, summer melon and citrus chile mint and remoulade vinaigrette. The second offering was Summer Stone fruit salad tossed with toasted pistachios and Pleasant Ridge cheese in champagne tangerine vinaigrette. The entre' was Texas Kobe Beef featuring slow roasted short ribs, flank and sirloin served with poblano mashed potatoes, tempura eggplant, ratatouille and piquillo peppers in a natural sauce. The portions were modestly sized and delectable leaving room for dessert. The *afters* would certainly be equally impressive but were declined. We were late for another type of dessert. And what awaited me far exceeded the elegance of my dining experience; it would prove to be a first course that would re-open my mind. And the mind altering event this evening was not a traditional offering. It came in the form of a movie. A movie whose title that appeared on the marquis was both intriguing and challenging. And whose content was life changing, in fact, as in my case, life-saving.

Entering the theater, the small crowd was much older than I had anticipated. Located in an area of Houston that catered to a younger bar clientele, tattoos and body piercings were more common than neck ties and heels. Nonetheless, enthusiasm for the flick was evident as an unsolicited endorsement was given by a distinguished older Houstonian as she called out, "What the *Bleep* Do You Know?" Amused by her own cleverness, she raised her wine glass as if to offer a toast and followed it with a wink and a smile. This was a prelude to the explanation for her enthusiasm. This was her third viewing in as many weeks and the experience had changed her life. As she rambled on about how the particulars of the movie cracked the foundation of her Southern Baptist beliefs. I looked at the faces in the crowd. Of those I viewed each had the appearance of successful, intelligent stewards of life. No peculiar individuals in this group, no psychos. The gathering had the look of a stockholder's meeting.

The theater was a converted playhouse that had been refitted with a screen and projection equipment. Tables and chairs replaced the traditional stadia seating. And ushers, both male and female, dressed in black slacks and black turtle necked shirts moved about as if they were dancing shadows, escorting the attendees to reserved seating. The table for my friends and me was in the center on a raised section of the proscenium. The view was clear and without obstruction. The drink orders were made and the lights lowered. The next couple of hours would forever impact my life.

My mind raced with possibilities. I made notes on anything I could find. ATM and retail receipts, the palm of my hand and several drink napkins recorded my experience. The beginning of the movie production flashed with electrical sparks and claps of thunder. Between the theatrics were the words: (flash and boom) IN THE BEGINIING WAS THE VOID (flash and boom) TEEMING WITH INFINITE POSSIBILITIES (flash and boom) OF WHICH YOU ARE ONE. I never considered myself as a possibility, I am real and certainly one of me is enough for this world. The narrator posed a couple of questions that created in me more than just a passing interest in the answers. Do multiple realities exist side by side? Have you ever seen yourself through the eyes of someone you have become? The chance meeting with friends proved to be mind changing.

For most Westerners, prayer is a part of one's life as a child. Its purpose, for the most, is that of a ceremonial prelude to dining, a bedtime ritual or a petition for help with a test for which a student is ill prepared. And to most it seemed to have little effect as to the taste of the food, or to the remedy of a bad situation. For most adult Westerners, prayer is reduced to a superstitious avoidance of certain phrases and the mindless utterance of others. All in all, prayer is summarily dismissed as ineffective and a bit superstitious. With the presumption that God knows one's heart and needs, prayer is abandoned as an activity that is deemed trite. And besides it is an awkward act to perform and embarrassing for the self conscious. To struggle for the correct wording and to avoid distraction is arduous and hopeless. It is difficult for one who is not gifted in theatrics to perform a part one does not feel. Added to that, *desired* answers to prayers are rarely experienced because of the absence in understanding the Mind of God and the power of Gratitude; the single emotion that affects change.

The rudiments of prayer and meditation, however, have value beyond belief. And its effects are visible to one's experience. Masaru Emoto's study of the effects thought and intent have on the development of ice crystals is stunning. His experiments using water from the Fujiwara dam placed in containers and then frozen were inconsistent with what one might expect. The growth of the ice crystals demonstrated stark variances. The vessels containing the water were first exposed to various conditions. And these conditions were defined by the spiritual and emotional state of the holder of the container. The water in the containers was then frozen and the ice crystals photographed and analyzed. Crystals that were not purposely affected with meditation or intent grew less elaborately than those blessed by a Zen Buddhist monk. And other ice crystals developed asymmetrically when exposed to negative intent and emotion. The differences were not slight, not open for interpretation; the variances were absolute and distinct.

Water has been presented as the most receptive of the four elements to thought; earth, wind, and fire are less so. And it was emphasized that it is no coincidence that the human body is affected by thought and intent as it is ninety percent water. It was proposed that our thoughts affect who we are and what we become. But then the suggestion was made, could one's thoughts affect others?

An independent study conducted in Washington, DC demonstrated the effect of prayer and meditation on humans. An assembly of meditative individuals met with the intent to reduce the crime rate of the Nation's capital to a predetermined level by simply willing it so. Their plan was straightforward; focus on the existing negative energy that promotes the intent to commit crime and intervene with a higher calling. The plan elicited a response from the city's mayor that it would take a blizzard in July to affect that type of change. The meditation continued around the clock and the goal of reducing the crime rate was achieved. The results of the conference documented a significant drop in the crime rate.

One cannot help but think of the times that emotions are allowed to run amuck. Deprecating thoughts that are the result of self loathing certainly can have an effect on one's confidence and health. Not to mention the far more common negative thoughts directed toward others and its effects on them, and one's self. The bond that apparently exists that links us together is intriguing. But how does it happen?

The presence of water and one's ability to cause change suggests a connectedness that cannot be ignored. And at this point, physics is introduced in the film as an explanation. There are many disciplines of physics that specialize in certain aspects of natural science. These specialties are grouped into three disciplines; one is Newtonian Physics which generally works well with larger objects such as planets, rockets and baseballs and their movements. Two is Relativity that introduces the relationship of gravity, time and the curvature of space; that which Einstein is famous for popularizing. And, three is Quantum Physics that deals primarily with the extremely small. And it is within the discipline of Quantum physics that connectedness is experienced and it is the most counter-intuitive field of physics.

By examining the realm of the very small, we find behavior that Einstein described as *spooky action at a distance.* Conventional wisdom and reason does not apply to one's experience at this level, and mathematics reveals the existence of eleven dimensions. Spooky actions, multi-dimensions and the power of thought is the stuff of which science fiction is made. Can any of this be true?

Entanglement is a term used in Quantum Physics to describe the way that particles of energy or matter can become linked, and to predictably interact with each other regardless of how far apart they are. To do something to one immediately affects the other, whether the two are inches or light years apart. This phenomenon creates an enigma with regard to logistics. Does the information travel incredibly fast from one to the other surpassing the speed of light, or are the two connected in a *spooky way* without regard to the distance of separation?

Entanglement suggests a connection, a physical link that is not apparent in human experience within the four dimensions. The origin of the universe, the Big Bang, marked the point of singularity when everything was one, and entanglement is the vestige of that singularity that still exist billions of years later as the galaxies rush apart. And it is this physical reality that makes feasible the principles of prayer and meditation and the effects one can have on the other.

Prayer, mediation and intent affect one's self and others. And the mode of communication for prayer, meditation and intent is at the quantum level. And it is at this level dimensions exist that are beyond our corporeal understanding.

This realization was my moment of insight. The seeds were planted in a fertile setting that permitted me to both accept the findings of science, and to trust the realm of the spiritual, the blending of science and spirituality as two threads of the same fabric. My faith, which had been at best on life support, was resuscitated. And I found the experience to be a breath of fresh air in that what I intuitively suspected as being true has tangible evidence to support it. That which I had discarded as useless, the simple act of prayer, was far more important than I had ever realized. I had discarded as useless the very mechanism that binds humans together as if we were Aspen trees of Colorado; sharing a common root system and an identical DNA. And to do that was to deny the very basics of life itself.

Superposition, another Quantum Physics concept, was introduced to explain the existence of alternate possibilities. The scene was a basketball court where dozens of basketballs bounced. The balls bounced at different heights and varying rates to demonstrate the world of Quantum physics. The bouncing balls represented several options to a proposed single query, a multiple choice approach to life. The narrator described the world of the very small as a world of possibilities. One where there were *waves* of options when one is not looking as with the bouncing balls. And a *single* reality when one focused as an observer, to see a single bouncing ball. Pick a ball, any ball was the suggestion. The single bouncing ball became reality, the world of possibilities changed to certainty.

When physicists measure a tiny particle, they find it in a particular place. However, demonstration shows that when they are not measuring the particle, it exists as a wave function, in all places it could possibly be – at the same time. Measuring or observing the particle collapses the wave function to one particular location. When we are not looking, multiple options exist. And when we do look, only one is apparent.

Incorporating prayer, meditation and intent with the idea of alternate possibilities and it then becomes apparent how outcomes can hinge on one's observation. As an adolescent when attending church services the pastor would often mention predestination. A preordained set of life events that one would experience because God knows all even before it happens. And that life is played out as God had written the script. Statements that suggested that God knew from the foundations of creation who and what one would become defined omniscience. Then at the close of the sermon when the invitation was given to make a decision to become a follower of Christ, the pastor would then mention freewill as if to suggest one has control over destiny. Did this suggest God's omnipotence to make course corrections? The contradiction created in me a crisis of faith and confusion. Either there was a set path for one's life, or there wasn't. Did God have a plan as if playing chess, staying one or two moves ahead of human cleverness and making course corrections? Or, better yet, are there multiple life scenarios playing out concurrently?

Superposition permits those multiple options and existence simultaneously. So it can be said that freewill does exist, and the decision is which life is chosen, or on what life one focuses. Then God can know the future, because there are many alternatives and an *unexpected* decision made by anyone of us does not disrupt the grand scheme of things. So humans are in control of their destinies in the decisions they make because God wills it so.

At this point in the film, I was mentally exhausted. I had more than enough to contemplate. It was then the concept of time was introduced. I had agonized about the past and I had hoped for a better future, all the while ignoring the *now* until this experience. The concept that time is a human invention because of a need to order events proved to crack my foundations. There has to be a start and an end to everything. And with that, a set of events in the middle that can be measured, or timed, so that life can be predictable. And to suggest that time does not exist and that everything is happening now is counter intuitive. But as the film suggests, nature – physics – has not a need for time. And if everything is happening now – not in the past or the future – then predestination, freewill and God knowing the future is easier to understand; because everything is happening at once.

*But, beloved, be not ignorant of this one thing, that
one day is with the Lord as a thousand years, and
a thousand years as one day.*      *2 Peter 3:8*

God is omnipresent. The difference in our perception and God's acuity is a matter of frequency – vibrations as suggested by String Physics. And the lower frequency at which humans experience their world is akin to slow motion in film making. The unseen bullet fired from the muzzle of a gun can be slowed to show its characteristics and path. So what originally happened in a split second is now an observed event. Humans see their world in slow motion; the spirit world sees it in real time; that is to say, no time.

# THE ILLUSION OF REALITY

*Healing may not be so much about getting better,*
*as about letting go of everything that isn't*
*you – all of the expectations,*
*all of the beliefs – and becoming who you are.*
Rachel Naomi Remen

Southwest flight 2626 landed in El Paso, Texas on a Sunday evening in mid August. The flight had been smooth and uneventful except for my extreme pain. The sharp throbbing in my right shoulder and arm was unbearable and had been so for over two weeks. Lifting my luggage and steering the rental car were difficult tasks to perform. And to concentrate on my responsibilities while ignoring this distraction was improbable. The physical experience mixed with the anxiety of possibly not accomplishing my mission worsened the circumstances.

Arriving at my scheduled assignment the following morning, the obvious signs of the malady caught the attention of my client. Grimacing in pain and the effects it had on my voice made those around me uncomfortable. And it was the client who, at that time acted with much more wisdom than I, called a physician. The physician made a preliminary diagnosis of a herniated disc between C6 and C7; between the sixth and seventh vertebrae of the cervical column. An MRI would confirm the existence of that condition.

The doctor explained that the soft-tissue discs between the bony vertebral bodies in the cervical spine are called intervertebral discs. These discs are composed of a soft gel-like center and a tough outer lining that surrounds the disc. The intervertebral disc creates a joint between each of the vertebral bodies that allows them to flex and extend, rotate slightly, and move with respect to one another. When the outer lining that surrounds the disc tears, the soft center squeezes out through the opening, creating a *herniated*, slipped, or ruptured disc. Each of these terms describes the same condition. You can imagine this process as similar to having a tube of toothpaste with a crack in it. If you exert pressure on the cracked tube, the toothpaste then flows out the crack.

He continued to describe the condition using a plastic model of a spine. Tears in the outer lining of the disc can be very painful by themselves. Once a tear has occurred, pressure from everyday activities, such as tilting one's head, can help to push the disc's gel-like center through the ruptured outer lining. When one has a tear in the outer lining, but the soft gel-like center has not been squeezed out of the center of the disc, then one will usually have pain in the neck only. However, if a torn outer lining is ruptured, the nucleus, or soft gel-like center irritates a nerve root, then pain can be experienced in the shoulders, arms and in your neck at the same time. This condition can cause different patterns of pain, numbness, and weakness in the body, depending upon where the slipped disc is located along your spine, and how the disc is pressing against the spinal cord and nerve roots.

When a nerve root or the spinal cord is being pinched, one may experience pain in the neck, and pain or numbness in one or both of your arms and hands. In severe cases, the muscles that are controlled by the nerve root that is being compressed by the disc herniation may become weak. The pain that is felt in the neck, back, and arms can come from a combination of a tear in the outer lining, from the pressure that the disc herniation puts on the nerve, or from irritation, inflammation and swelling within the nerve.

The diagnosis of a herniated cervical disc begins with a complete physical examination of the neck, arms and lower extremities. And it was the orthopedic surgeon who conducted this examination that said surgery was the only option to correct the condition. The doctor examined my neck for flexibility, range of motion, and the presence of certain signs that suggested that the nerve roots or spinal cord were affected by the disc herniation. This involved testing the strength of my muscles and checking my reflexes to make sure that they are still working normally, and they were not.

The surgeon then ordered a set of x-rays. The x-rays were normal because the disc is composed of soft tissue and does not show up on the x-ray. In situations where a herniated disc is a likely the cause of symptoms, doctors will order an MRI. And that was what the surgeon did. An appointment was scheduled for an imaging of the cervical column.

An MRI scan is very useful in determining where disc herniations have occurred and where the nerve roots or spinal cord are being compressed. A CT scan is often used to evaluate the bony anatomy in the cervical spine, which can show how much space is available for the nerve roots and spinal cord within the spinal canal. The nerve roots exit the spinal canal through a bony tunnel called the neuroforamen, and it is at this point that the nerve roots are especially vulnerable to compression by disc herniations.

A CT scan or an MRI is often not ordered until a decision has been made to proceed with surgery. And this was the presumption of the surgeon that I would agree to the medical intervention. Studies have shown that many people with *normal* necks have evidence of significant cervical disc herniations on MRI scans, and these people do not have any symptoms of neck pain. Therefore, MRI's are usually ordered only when the diagnosis is unclear, or after it becomes apparent that the patient is not going to get better with non-surgical options and the surgeon needs to determine what type of surgery is best to relieve the symptoms.

Surgery for cervical disc herniations is offered as an option for people who have evidence of muscle weakness that is being caused by nerve root or spinal cord compression. This is because muscle weakness is a definite sign that the nerves are being injured and relieving the pressure on the nerves is more of an urgent priority. And as if the pain were not enough, simple acts of lifting luggage or steering an automobile were intimidating tasks. Surgery was scheduled three weeks out, after completion of my scheduled assignments.

For some reason unknown to me at the time, the haste in which the decision was made troubled me. It was more than the fear of going under the knife; it was awareness that there is something I have not yet experienced, or learned, or understood. The all-or-nothing conclusion from a singular source to opt for a solution whose epaulets are stitches and scars seemed to be a compromise to a more divine answer. And as it is in Westerner thought, I was quick to dismiss my uneasiness as the ramblings of a coward.

Waiting on line to pay for a newspaper at the local bookstore, a person in front of me placed an arm load of books onto the counter. The clerk totaled the purchase and the customer was short of available funds. Counting her cash and reviewing the cost of each book, she decided to not purchase two of her selections. Turning to apologize for causing the delay, she then completed the transaction and it was then my attention was drawn to her discarded selections. Circumstance and coincidence were concepts that I was learning to pay closer attention to as opportunities to act. I purchased the two books; each had as its theme, belief and healing.

***

Science and religion are not in fundamental opposition in India, as in the West. They are seen as parts of the same great search for truth and enlightenment. That search has inspired the sages of Hinduism, Buddhism, and Jainism; a search that is measured in millennia. And far too often the mention of those religious disciplines offends those in the West that are unfamiliar with the fundamental beliefs of each.

The Hindu scientific approach of understanding external reality depends on also understanding the divine. In all Hindu traditions the Universe is said to precede not only humanity but also the gods. Fundamental to Hindu concepts of time and space is the notion that the external world is a product of the creative play of *Maya*, which is defined as *illusion*. Accordingly, the world as we know it is not solid and real but illusionary. And the universe is in constant change with many levels of reality; the task is to find release, *moksha*, from the bonds of time and space. The Prashasta Pada:

> *After a cycle of universal dissolution, the Supreme Being decides to recreate the cosmos so that we souls can experience worlds of shape and solidity. Very subtle atoms begin to combine, eventually generating a cosmic wind that blows heavier*

*and heavier atoms together. Souls depending on their karma earned in previous world systems, spontaneously draw to themselves atoms that coalesce into an appropriate body.*

Hindu cosmology is aligned with modern physics as it envisions the universe as having a cyclical nature. At the cusp of two cycles, the ending of one cycle and the beginning of the next, is called *kalpa*, and is brought about by Shiva's dance. Rebirth follows destruction.

The Western world lives in the past, placing an extreme value on the historical prospective. India is rooted in a timeless universe of eternal return. Everything that is happening has already happened many times before. These recurring happenings may have taken on different guises. Deep meditation and ascetic practices are both characteristics and traits of the people that gave rise to Hinduism. Those that felt that they have gained an insight into the nature of reality followed these practices. Science uses a heuristic method, problem solving by experimentation, which requires objective proof of mathematical theories. Yet both have found their way to propose similar scenarios for the creation and outcomes of the universe.

The Western world has only recently *discovered* what the ancient mystics have known for millennia. These astute individuals had an intuitive understanding of the origin, nature, methods, and limits of human knowledge. And they also had an awareness of the natural order of the universe. Their unification of the spiritual and the physical was not difficult for them; the apparent separation is simply an illusion.

Western science has only recently developed an understanding that the universe is extremely old. In 1965, the temperature of the universe was measured for the first time. The purpose of the testing was to determine the age of the Cosmos. The results estimated the age as 15 billion years old.

In the ancient literature of India one does not find such precise figures. Instead there are analogies such as the following.

*Imagine an immortal eagle flying over the Himalayas only once every 1,000 years; it carries a feather in its beak and each time it passes, it lightly brushes the tops of the gigantic mountain peaks. The amount of time it would take the eagle to completely erode the mighty Himalayas is said to be the age of the present manifestation of the universe.*

Such a conception of time, without specific numbers on which Westerners expect, which predates modern science by thousands of years, is thought to be remarkable. Especially when it is compared to how slow realization of Western science and religion is to the possibility of a less humanlike time scale.

Eastern mysticism and quantum physics are also remarkably similar. The mystics have always rejected *existence* independent of human observation. The notion of a mechanistic nature churning out independent pieces of reality is counter to the blending of the physical and the spiritual. Reality does not consist of separate things, but is an indescribable, interconnected oneness.

One's experience is but a brief disturbance in a universal ocean of existence. *Maya* is the illusion that the world of separate objects and people is the *only* reality. For the mystics this manifestation is real, but it is a fleeting reality; it is a mistake, although a natural one, to believe that Maya represents a fundamental reality. Each person, each physical object, from the perspective of eternity is like a brief, disturbed drop of water from an unbounded ocean.

The goal of enlightenment is to understand this, or better stated, to experience this: to see intuitively that the distinction between me and the universe is a false dichotomy. That is the distinction that an individual is separate and apart from the Universe is simply an error in understanding how things are connected. The same distinction between consciousness and physical matter, between mind and body, is the result of an unenlightened perspective.

*Maya* is illusion, and what mankind understands to be reality is, in fact, the dream of Brahma. And the dream of Brahma is the Universe. Brahma is the creator and great magician who through imaginings creates. The dream itself is maintained by Vishnu, the Preserver, who uses *maya* to spin the complex **web** that we know as reality. The world itself is not an illusion, only our perception of the world. We then suppose the universe to be made up of a multitude of objects, structures and events. The theory of maya asserts that all things are one. Rational categories such as exist in Western thought are mere fabrications of the human mind and have no ultimate reality.

Western science is now confirming ancient traditions that an intelligent field of energy exist that bathes all of creation. And just as with the **web** that Vishnu spins to create *reality,* this field of energy serves as a vessel for all that is, or has been, or will ever be. It also provides a gateway for inner emotions of humanness to integrate with creation itself. And more remarkably, it functions as a mirror to re-create our most heartfelt intent in physical reality. One's expectation creates creation. And as human experience pushes the boundaries of the heavens and the limits of the quantum world, and as we peer further into space and deeper into the microscopic realm, matter is created because we expect it to be where we look.

All matter originates from this field as disturbances – wrinkles and folds – in the fabric of this **web**. And our thoughts – emotions – affect these disturbances.

The concept of an interactive Universe is counter intuitive to many. The belief that humans affect change was an idea that confused even Einstein. And he was not alone. The scientific community of the West for most of the twentieth century held to a concept that life was subject to the laws of nature and not an influential part of them. In concert with the scientific community, major Western religions held a similar position. Religious tenets promoted theologies that a supreme entity was either unable, or unwilling, to break from the rules because of divine laws. And that a prayer of supplication that was not favorably answered was still in accordance to the will of God. If the beliefs of each individual govern how each lives their lives and what outcomes are experienced, the focus then becomes how to affect one's beliefs.

Each discipline, science and religion, offers more than just scattered hints of our place in the Cosmos. Quantum physics has demonstrated that a particle can be in two places at the same time. And even though they are separated by large distances, one iteration reacts instantaneously and predictably when the other is affected. Distance, and the time it takes to react are immediate, that is to say, faster than *nature's* speed limit – the speed of light. And not only do the separated entities *feel* the effects of the other, the change is retroactive to the particles past – as if the change has always been.

Humans, as is everything, is a conglomeration of particles. These particles have the same characteristics and properties of those mentioned previously; and if the particles that comprise us are capable of such actions, why not we. We are! It is a matter of belief. Belief that has influenced our thoughts in our science books has limited our experience to what can be measured and predicted. And that in itself is not all bad if there remains an opportunity to permit intuitiveness. And where one might find an avenue for intuitiveness, in say, religion, that option is squelched because faith and dogma are often confused as closed issues with nothing new to discover; and questioning either is not permitted.

Belief may be the most powerful aspect of humanness. As with Vishnu's spinning the web of illusion and humans interpreting their reality in that web, belief then governs how one thinks, how one acts, and how one values their existence. Accepting that realization then enables one to access the power of belief in one's life. And then by *feeling* that belief in one's heart it ennobles our thoughts to the certainty of our intent.

The human heart is many times more electrically active than the human brain. And it is the electrical and magnetic properties of the heart that permits one's beliefs to interact with the physical world. It is this interaction that is at a level that has been limited in discussion to the religious communities that is now been demonstrated in the scientific world of quantum physics.

An experiment conducted in the 1909 by Geoffrey Ingram Taylor demonstrated the properties of light, specifically photons. A machine that would provide the source of the photons – light – would be placed in front of a screen with a single slit. This machine would emit a single photon. And predictably when it passed through the slit, a single point of light was viewed on the projection board. When the screen was modified with several slits, a single photon was emitted and the result was not so predictable. The single photon passed through all of the slits at the same time. Acting as a wave of light when multiple slits were present, and as a single particle when only one slit was present was truly a strange occurrence. The enigma was how a photon can be several places at the same time, as with the wave analogy, and yet still be a single particle. Additionally, how did the particle know to react as a wave as opposed to a single particle?

In 1998, this experiment was re-conducted with more sophisticated equipment. The basic results were the same with one major exception. The more the particles were watched, the greater the diversity of their actions. It was as if the photons reacted to human consciousness and responded accordingly. And that was the conclusion that was drawn by the scientist conducting the experiment. We are made of the same stuff that was observed in the experiment and the catalyst for change was the observations of the scientist. What then would prevent our affecting the particles that make us who we are if in fact we are the observers in our own experiment in living?

The reality without illusion is that we must become that which we want to experience. And we experience what we believe. Experience is that which we have learned and can logically explain. And experience is that which we simply know to be. And the two are important and can lead to miracles in our lives. To logically change our minds we must first have been convinced that there are other ways of thinking. And that this convincing leads us to new conclusions. With new ways of thinking often comes a miracle in our lives. The understandings of the components of the miracle are less important than the acceptance of it in our lives.

***

The thought of surgery was becoming less and less a desirable option. The more I researched other clinical options the more I grew suspect of hidden agendas. Not so much hidden agendas as much as provincial thinking. A surgeon's recommendation was surgery. A pain management specialist's recommendation was periodic injections. A chiropractor's recommendation was realignment and regularly scheduled adjustments. All in all, each promoted what they knew, and that is to be expected.

With the realization that one promotes one's skills, I then took more seriously the idea that if one's thoughts affect one's life, and if one's observation affects reality, why would any of the medical interventionalists be needed? Why not contemplate another option and why not meditate on a better existence?

The modality of prayer is based on feeling. When one feels the feeling within their bodies as if a prayer has already been answered, then the heartfelt emotion creates the energy that is mirrored in the physical world at the quantum level. Western science is demonstrating under laboratory conditions that the quantum field does, in fact, reflect or mirror the language that we speak in terms of healing thought, feeling and emotion.

The medicine-less hospitals in China, demonstrate the power of the spiritual technology of thought, feeling and emotion. The practitioners are trained to unify those three separate, yet related experiences. As they are taught to unify those experiences within their bodies, what we find is that the physical world beyond their bodies responds to that force.

A woman who had been diagnosed with an inoperable bladder cancer had a tumor that was three inches in diameter. Western doctors said that they couldn't help her. She resorted to an option that most would consider a death wish. She found herself at the medicine-less hospital in China where she was trained to modify her lifestyle. Nourishing her body in new ways, navigating gentle life-affirming movements, breathing life-affirming breath were lifestyle changes that were made. As she implemented those changes, she was in effect preparing herself to assist the practitioners with thoughts, feelings and emotions.

The three practitioners felt the feeling as if she had already been healed and in two minutes and 40 seconds her body mirrored that quality of emotion. An ultra sound recorded the happening. As the practitioners chanted their gratitude, the cancer reversed itself as others watched and recorded the miracle.

The process only appears to be a miracle. To those who understand thought, feeling and emotion they see it as a literal technology, a spiritual technology. It's a technology that requires very little special training. The special tools that are required, everyone possess within one's body. It's simply the awareness of the power and the empowering nature of thought, feeling and emotion.

Having been exposed to the concept of seeing one's self from where one wants to be, and in this situation that was healed. I imagined the bulging disc retracting from the crack in its protective covering. I envisioned it as if it were a movie. The words I repeated over and over as I *saw* the disc moving back into the proper placement was, "I am glad it is done! I am grateful it is gone!"

This *intervention* did not take weeks, or days to affect; the improvement, the healing of my condition took minutes and the pain left my body.

# FLYING MONKEYS

*Finding myself to exist in the world, I believe I shall, in some shape or other, always exist.*
Benjamin Franklin

The annual spring break vacation was typical in the sense that the restlessness of the backseat drivers weighed heavily on my patience. The smell of snacks, drinks and other odors coupled with the constant bickering of the siblings made me crazy. The traffic on the Dan Ryan Expressway was unbelievably heavy and at times the car would come to a complete stop. If only the noise from the rear of the car would ebb and flow with the traffic, at least that would provide some periods of relief. It was at that moment, the younger child asked for quiet. And his countenance changed from a tired, unruly passenger to one transfixed on something beyond the car and the present. And what happened next was not typical of a spring break vacation.

The four year old spoke to us, to someone, or to himself as he described living as an adult in Chicago. Staring through the passenger window, he repeatedly said he had been here before and that he had worn a suit, a Sunday suit, the kind the pastor wears. He said his work was performed in an office in a large building where *things* were made. And his office was at the top of the stairs and had windows so that he could watch the ones who did dirty-work. The cars were plain and black. And it was a time when a lot people stood on line to get food and many went to bed hungry. He remembered going to the movies and watching monkeys fly and listening to a song about a rainbow. For several minutes he quoted detail that was beyond his knowledge. At times he would sit silently staring, not at anything in particular, just staring as if he saw a world beyond the obvious. His blank stare turned into a slight smile as he turned and resumed his playful banter with his older brother, and never mentioned that collection of memories again.

Taking exit number 52A onto the West Congress Parkway and then to South Michigan Avenue, traffic once again came to a standstill. Anxious to get the family to the Field Museum of Natural History, my attention was drawn to an old Volvo Sedan. The weather that is characteristic of Chicago winters had obviously taken its toll. The tired car was worn and rusted and it seemed the dozens of bumper stickers had a more practical use of holding it together rather than communicating opinion and prejudice. There was one that stood out. And it spoke volumes as it simply stated: *Born Again? Many Times!* And under that in smaller text was: *Reincarnation Is Having A Comeback!* I looked to the back seat at the four year old and thought the unthinkable; did he have a previous life?

***

I began to pay closer attention to the notion of reincarnation. At first, I broached the subject in casual conversation with friends and family. And when one discusses reincarnation the subject is either met with skepticism, or guarded interest. And only when one researches those that have either had experiences, or those that have conducted credible studies, only then does the subject become more than just mere fantasy. And that was what I did, I read about those that had spent their lives researching past lives.

The scientific community still marginalizes most work that even hints at realities beyond our own. This marginalization manifests itself as prejudice, a blatant intolerance that has no limits because belief in the possibility of multiple lives would compromise traditional tenets of Western society. The knowledge and realization that if one does not *get it right* in this life, that one will have an opportunity *in the next,* opens the doors of possibilities for the individual, and closes the doors for those who want ultimate control.

Western religions that place an emphasis on a single-life opportunity has leverage in dictating prescribed standards of conduct and eternal consequences of actions. The presumed guardianship of the soul by these organizations would fall by the wayside if the parishioners were suddenly made knowledgeable that sinning may not damn one to perdition's flames. The absence of a final judgment before God without the alternatives of reward or punishment renders the authority of religion impotent. So, at the worst, reincarnation may simply mandate the repeating of an opportunity to re-live what one does not *get right* the first time. All in all, surrendering control to the individual is not the stuff of which pious bureaucracy is made.

Governmental concerns regarding a populace that believes in multiple lives would also cause problems. Those individuals that seemingly have made a mess of their lives could be tempted to opt for an early transition to hopefully fare better in the next life. Poor health, dismal finances, tortured relationships; all could be reasons for quitting. Disingenuous individuals could use this exit strategy for personal gratification, that is, to inflict recourse on whom and whatever they deem deserving. And the civil authorities would then be left to mend the broken and encourage the disheartened.

These fears cloud the understanding of what ancient cultures have known and respected. While there is no judgment in what one believes – it is what it is; there is, however, a given presumption that each person seeks a level of understanding to facilitate growth in one's lives. It could be said that those who make the decision to transition because of circumstance, are only following their life's destiny. And judgments made by religious groups, governmental agencies, or by individuals is a part of the same prejudice that affects research into this subject.

Clinging to a control mindset of which mainstream science, religion and politics currently holds creates risks in becoming what is best described by George Orwell:

> *...smelly little orthodoxies...contending for our souls!*

There are however cultures, groups and individuals that are far more intuitive and knowledgeable than the so called experts. Everyone, for the most part, has heard of the concept of reincarnation. And, even in America, one of three individuals believes in past and future lives; many of whom are Christians and defy their church's tenets in doing so.

*\*\*\**

Credible individuals have made the doctrine of reincarnation their life's work. One such person was a Christian fundamentalist, and conducted his avocation while sleeping. The *Sleeping Prophet*, as he is called, channeled thousands of people. His ability to read past-lives and describing in detail their existences confounded those that bore witness to these events. The information retrieved from this type of experience is called *retro-cognition*. These readings resulted in an extreme variety of information; previous happenings in an individual's life, accidents, traumas; as well as ancient history, including earth's geologic past. Details of mysterious tribes and lost civilizations that predate recorded history teased those that listened or read the revelations. While placing himself into a trance, Edgar Cayce would not only give incredible details previously listed, he also related how those experiences affected the health of his clients.

Cayce was born on March 18, 1877, on a farm near Hopkinsville, Kentucky. As an elementary school student, he found it difficult to remember his spelling words, in fact, he was quite deficient scholastically. And one day as he was sitting near a wooded area reading his Bible, a figure appeared to him that would be best described as an angel. The figure was clothed in white and possessed a bright countenance. The *angel* asked Edgar what he most wanted to do in life and Cayce responded by saying to help others. The angel instructed Edgar to sleep and all would be well. He did sleep using as a pillow his spelling book. And later he awoke to a new life; a life of service to others and as an exceptional speller – knowing all of the words in his book.

Edgar Cayce was not a good student and this makes the circumstances more remarkable. He was known by his contemporaries as an unassuming man. In his waking state he was shy, quiet and lacked the presence one might presume of someone of his notoriety. He became renowned for the scholarly manner in which he spoke while in a trance; using terminology and technical terms in precise context.

Cayce's medical knowledge in his sleep state was phenomenal. And without formal training and education in that discipline, those that witnessed his readings were amazed. He would frequently suggest the prescription of drugs that were not yet developed, or marketed, or had long been discontinued. Cayce's use of the English language in his awakened state was unremarkable. But in his sleep state not only would he use impeccable oratory skills in English, he did the same in over twenty four different languages.

Cayce believed there was a cure for every health problem. He was not an advocate for operations; believing that surgery was much overworked. Cayce's holistic approach to medicine transcends the modern day definition. He believed that a person was composed of body, mind and spirit, and that trinity is One. He believed the cells of the body have their own consciousness. And it is the sum total of the awareness of the cells that comprises one's total consciousness. This resulted in his belief that one's health issues were carried over from the previous life.

Cayce died more than 65 years ago, on January 3, 1945. The focus of his readings was that of discovering one's mission in life, developing intuition, exploring ancient mysteries, and taking responsibility for one's health. For him it wasn't nearly as important who one once was, or even what one once did, as it was to focus on the present. And by focusing on the present, to take on the opportunities and challenges that are faced in this time, in this place, right now.

***

Dr. Ian Stevenson held the positions of the head of the Department of Psychiatry at the University of Virginia, and the Director of the Division of Perceptual Studies at the University of Virginia. His work that covered the span of forty years provided scientific documentation of past life memories of children. From all over the world, over 3000 cases were chronicled in his files. Skeptics and scholars agree that these cases offer the best evidence yet for reincarnation. The following is his obituary written by Emily Williams Kelly Ph.D.:

*Ian P. Stevenson, M.D., died February 8, 2007 in Charlottesville, Virginia, at age 88.*

*Dr. Stevenson is known worldwide for his research, conducted over more than 40 years, on cases of the reincarnation type and other evidence for survival after death. Born in Montreal, Canada, on October 31, 1918, he was educated at St. Andrew's University in Scotland and McGill University in Montreal, and he received his medical degree from McGill in 1943, earning an award for the highest aggregate in all subjects forming the medical curriculum. After a brief period of research in biochemistry, Stevenson, dissatisfied with its reductionism, looked for a way to study what he considered 'something closer to the whole human being.' In the late 1940s, therefore, he joined a group at New York Hospital and began research in psychosomatic medicine, particularly on the effects of stress and strong emotions on physical symptoms. This work eventually led him to training in psychiatry and psychoanalysis, and in 1957, at the young age of 38, he was appointed Professor and Chairman of the Department of Psychiatry at the University of Virginia.*

*Long periods of seclusion due to a childhood illness helped foster his lifelong habit of voracious reading.*

*In 1935 he started keeping a list of every book he read, and by 2003 it numbered 3,535 books. His extraordinarily wide reading in history in particular showed him the transience of ideas and convictions once considered immutable, and he strongly resisted the temptation of many scientists to 'accept current knowledge as forever fixed., As a result, throughout his life he experienced the considerable obstacles confronting a scientist who wishes to conduct and publish unorthodox research. After he published a paper in 1957 questioning the orthodox Freudian view that human personality is determined by early childhood experiences, a colleague asked him whether he could walk the streets unarmed.*

*Dissatisfied with the reductionism of both biochemistry and Freudian psychoanalysis, Dr. Stevenson began to search for more satisfactory theories of the origin of individual differences and the development of personality. In the early 1950s, encouraged by a meeting with Aldous Huxley, he became one of the first academics in America to investigate the effects of psychedelic drugs in a psychiatric context. One experience with LSD induced what he described as 'a mystical experience,' in which he experienced three days of 'perfect serenity' and the sense that 'I could never be angry again.' As it happens, that didn't work out, but the memory of it persisted as something to hope for.*

*Experiences such as this deepened his dissatisfaction with prevailing theories of mind and body and eventually led him to undertake extensive reading in the literature of psychical research about extrasensory perception and a wide variety of experiences suggesting survival after death, such as apparitions, near-death experiences and deathbed visions, and mediumship. He eventually conducted and published research in all these areas, but it was the discovery in obscure publications of numerous scattered reports of young children who seemed to have memories of a previous life that led to the research that he pioneered and for which he is now best known. In 1961 he took his first field trip, to India and Sri Lanka (then Ceylon), to study at first hand the reported previous life memories of young children. After this first trip, Chester Carlson, the inventor of the Xerox machine, funded additional trips, and when Carlson died in 1968 he left funds for research and an endowed chair, sufficient to allow Dr. Stevenson to resign from his clinical and administrative duties and devote himself full-time to research. In addition, Dr. Stevenson was able to found the Division of Personality (now Perceptual) Studies, the only university-based research unit in the world devoted to the study of previous life memories, near-death experiences, and related phenomena.*

*Over the next 35 years, Dr. Stevenson traveled extensively throughout the world – sometimes*

*logging an average of 55,000 miles a year –
identifying and studying nearly 3000 cases in
Asian and Western cultures. His research was
characterized by an almost obsessive attention
to detail and corroboration of reports with
interviews with numerous firsthand witnesses as
well as with documents such as birth certificates
and postmortem reports. His empirical approach
made him deeply skeptical of purported accounts
of previous lives obtained by hypnosis or past life
regression. He kept a file in his office which he
labeled 'Extravagant Claims,' containing numerous
Thomas Jeffersons, Mary Magdalenes, Napoleons,
and Josephines, and he would speculate amusingly
to colleagues about what would happen if they were
all to be locked in a room together.*

*Dr. Stevenson was the author of over 300
publications, including 14 books. In his publications
on cases of the reincarnation type, he identified
numerous recurring and cross-cultural patterns,
including the ages when children would typically
speak about their memories (beginning at about
2-3 years and ending by 7 or 8), the mode of death
of the previous personality (often violent or sudden),
and unusual behaviors (including phobias,
unusual skills or interests, and gender confusion
when the previous life was that of the opposite
sex). His magnum opus, however, is a 2-volume,
2268-page monograph reporting over 200 cases in
which highly unusual birthmarks or birth defects*

*of the child corresponded with marks, usually fatal wounds, on the previous person.*

*Dr. Stevenson saw this research as indicating a possible third factor, in addition to genetics and environment, in the development of human personality. His emphasis, however, was always on the evidence, and his greatest frustration was not that other scientists dismissed his interpretations of the evidence, but that most of them did so without even bothering to read the evidence that he had so painstakingly assembled.*

*In 1982 Dr. Stevenson was instrumental in the founding of the Society for Scientific Exploration, an organization for scientists involved in areas of research challenging many assumptions of contemporary science. Despite his unorthodox interests, he was the embodiment of academic rectitude in both dress and demeanor; but his single-minded, serious devotion to his life's work was tempered by a wry, dry sense of humor. Commenting, for example, that he was 'apprehensive' but not afraid of death, he said: "I have a feeling I'm going to be confronted with memories, some of which I won't like and would like to expunge. But I do wonder, what parents could possibly want me as a baby?"*

*Dr. Stevenson's first wife, Octavia, died in 1983. His second wife, Margaret, survives him, as do his brother,*

*Dr. Kerr L. White of Charlottesville, his sister, Edith Meisner of Knowlton, Quebec, his nieces Margo and Susan, and nephews Preston, Geoffrey, and Mark. He had no children, but he leaves numerous younger colleagues inspired, trained, and encouraged in their own careers by him.*

*Written by Emily Williams Kelly, Ph.D.*
*Research Assistant Professor*
*Division of Perceptual Studies*
*University of Virginia Health System*

Dr. Stevenson has documented the strongest cases of reincarnation. Working primarily with young children and their remembering details about their past lives, his work leaves little room for the skeptic. Most of the documented cases were of children that live in India and in the Middle East. Dr. Stevenson's interest began with a child's ability to talk. And when a child referred to *another family* and provided details and names of relatives, he would then become intrigued. Other signs of interest would be emotions that would be consistent with a past life such as having an affinity toward a particular religion or social class. Occasionally, the reincarnated would insist on being taken home – back to the former family, even under the threat of punishment for making the request. And much stranger is the phenomenon of *xenoglossy* which is the ability to speak and understand a language that has not been learned by conventional methods. These characteristics documented the cases Stevenson deemed as credible.

There were times when an apparent case of reincarnation was locally publicized and arrangements made to reunite family members. In most of these cases Dr. Stevenson conducted post-meeting interviews, and with some trepidation. Other times, however, he orchestrated the reunion and placed extreme controls to assure accurate, uncompromised documentation and to make sure the reporting was fair.

There were 250 extremely strong cases for reincarnation where each child made as many as 40 specific statements about a past life that proved to be true. There were thousands of cases where this same statement process was followed with a lesser number of statements but with accurate information. The child would identify the former relatives. There were even attempts made by Stevenson to try to trick the child with disguises; and the child would act either amused or annoyed by the ruse and react appropriately. Many gave personal, intimate details that only the past-life person could possibly have known; such as with the location of where money was hidden in the house or a secret known by no one but a dead relative.

In addition to the physical bodies of the reincarnated were the *marks* those bodies carried. Dr. Stevenson's research concluded that birthmarks, or deformities, provide a clue as to how the previous life ended. This provides another very convincing proof of reincarnation. There are several cases where Dr. Stevenson has investigated the autopsy records of the previous life, and then matched up the photographs showing how they died with the child's birthmarks. In many of these cases, there was a memory of being shot, or stabbed, or struck that resulted in death. And the resulting birthmarks of the child mirrored the entry and exit wounds of a gunshot victim, or a birthmark in the shape of a stab wound, and a larger, more extensive marking indicating a more extreme incident.

A similar case documented a boy with detailed memories of a past life. The boy's chest was covered with what looked like a scattering of red blotches. Dr. Stevenson researched the previous-life person and discovered he had experienced a shotgun blast to the chest. The photograph of the victim's chest displaying the entry wounds of the pellets matched the red, splotchy areas on the boy.

Dr. Stevenson conducted what is arguably a controlled study of this phenomenon. And he has resulted far more cases as hoaxes, or unsupportable, that others with less integrity would have reason to rationalize. He held those studies that survived extreme scrutiny as his evidence. Dr. Stevenson has left the planet, as has Edgar Cayce. There are however others that are conducting current research. Dr. Brian Weiss, Denise Linn, Alberto Villoldo, Ph.D., and many more that continue to document what, once again, the ancients knew. And what did the ancients know?

The Akashic Record is an *etheric place* where our collective and individual memories are stored. Surviving from ancient times, it has been considered either a myth, or a fact. Yet, the belief in this repository, also called the *Book of Life,* has been a part of our world's cultures for centuries. Like many ancient stories that were considered too farfetched to have any credence, this belief has been labeled by some as implausible.

But, consider the mythical city of Troy. It was considered a fabled concoction of an ancient writer to tell a tale. It was labeled a fictional place for millennia. And only after considering the writings of Homer as a literal source of fact were enlightened archaeologists led to the location of the fabled city. Using detailed directions in the text of the *Iliad and the Odyssey,* the lost city was found. Could there be a similar set of directions yet undiscovered that would create the same experience with this mystery? And more importantly, does this *place* hint as to where we go when we transition, and what we may elect to export into the next life? Regardless, we are then left to ponder its existence as that of a fictional tale, or a divine place.

The Akashic Field performs as a data warehouse for every single thought, action and response we have ever had regarding all of life's situations. We all have a past. We each have a history in this life, and in a previous existence. And it is the combining of what we know in the present life with what we can access in the past that explains who we are. Regardless of the number of lives one may have lived, the past can be instrumental in how the current life is lived and how it evolves. Although one is often reminded by friends, clinicians, clergy and therapists to not live in the past, one's history can provide much needed assistance is shaping one's future.

Tapping into the Akashic Field can serve as a diagnostic tool for assessing one's current life. Reviewing events, patterns and beliefs in previous lives can shed light on how one makes decisions in the present. This *field of dreams* holds all of our memories and thus holds who we are. And it simply awaits our tapping of its resources to make our lives what we envision them to be.

The Western world is haunted by a delusion that humankind was created from nothing, and that each is given one opportunity to live life. The concept that one does not begin with birth confounds those that rely on ego. And for those that depend on *smelly little orthodoxies that contend for one's soul* for guidance and direction, they, too, are lost. The voices of one's past echoes throughout the ages begging the question; how many times will I exist? The answer is infinite. We all have a feeling from time to time of an existence beyond our finger tips. Whether it is in a dream performing a concerto, or with a glance of a passing stranger that seems all too familiar, one senses that this is not a first passing through a cycle of life. In fact what we know and how well we use that knowledge is an accumulation of experience that began beyond this current incarnation. So, it is now easier to understand how a four year old from the rear seat of a car can recall details of a life in a strange city where he saw flying monkeys.

# WHEN A CHILD CRIES

*One need not be a chamber to be haunted;*
*One need not be a house;*
*The brain has corridors surpassing*
*Material place*
Emily Dickinson

The conference at Milsaps College in Jackson, Mississippi was a gathering of business managers, mostly male and completely competitive. Positioning, both professionally and psychologically, made the day sessions stressful and the evening gatherings comical. What one lacked in skills, knowledge or experience was adjusted with bravado, booze and backslapping. And the most obnoxious was the most faint-hearted. What I didn't expect was Jayson's response to my question regarding the Myrtles Plantation.

Jayson was only two years removed from his experience as a Mississippi State football player. Taking the field as an offensive lineman, he was by anyone's definition an imposing presence. And he continued that presence as a facade after his gridiron days by projecting a rough and tough demeanor. The playing field became leveled, or tilted toward vulnerability, as the discussion of the plantation continued. He laughed more, although nervously, as he motioned for me to follow him to the terrace. There he confided in me his deepest fear.

With a backdrop of Magnolias and the fluttering of fireflies he told his story. It was a story of fraternity brothers taking a road trip to drink and party. He did not remember who suggested as their destination the Myrtles Plantation, but nonetheless he found himself standing under the live oaks at a 200 year old mansion. It was at this point his rowdy voice broke as he all but whispered his experience. Checking in, the group was given a complimentary tour of the mansion, complete with history and folklore. Although he and his burly buddies made light of their uneasiness, he then said what followed scared him beyond belief.

Arriving mid-afternoon, he made the decision to go to his room and take a nap – advanced rest for the late-night party to follow. Before he told me the details of the experience, he verbally confirmed his manhood and qualified his intrepidness when facing a challenge. He then said what happened next compromised those standards. Reclining on the bed he drifted off to sleep. It was shortly after that he awoke with the blanket pulled tightly around his neck; not so tight that it caused him difficulty in breathing, but just enough to awaken him. He then said that at the same time something rubbed his legs. He then placed his hand on my forearm and firmly squeezed to imitate the intensity of the rubbing he had felt.

If he were exaggerating his grip to embellish his story by twofold then a fraction of the pressure would have still been noticeable. His first response was to scream, and he did. The second response was to run from the room, and he did. And the third response was to leave the plantation, and he did that, too. His final comment to me was that he would never return to the Myrtles.

I promised to keep his tale confidential and I immediately went to my room and researched the history of the plantation. Surfing

Internet sites I retrieved several comments and items that made reference to Chloe, the spirit of a murdered slave girl that massages the legs of guests and then tucks them in for the night. Exactly the story Jayson had told. I then read more regarding Chloe.

According to the story, the troubles that led to the haunting began in 1817 when Sarah Mathilda married Clark Woodruff. Sara Matilda had given birth to two daughters and was carrying a third child when an event took place that still haunts the Myrtles today.

Clark Woodruff had a reputation in the region for integrity with men and with the law, but was also known for being promiscuous. While his wife was pregnant with their third child, he started an intimate relationship with one of his slaves. This particular girl, whose name was Chloe, was a household servant. Who, while she hated being forced to give in to Woodruff's sexual demands, realized that if she didn't, she could be sent to work in the fields, which was the most brutal of a slave's work.

Eventually, Woodruff tired of Chloe and chose another girl with whom to carry on. Chloe feared the worst, sure that she was going to be sent to the fields, she began eavesdropping on the Woodruff family's private conversations, all the while dreading the mention of her name. One day, the Judge caught her at this and ordered that one of her ears be cut off to teach her a lesson and to put her in her place. After that time, she always wore a green turban around her head to hide the ugly scar that the knife had left behind.

What actually happened next is still unclear. Some claim that what occurred was done so that the family would just get sick so that Chloe could nurse them back to health and earn the Judge's gratitude. In this way, she would be safe from ever being returned to the fields. Others say that her motives were not so pure though and that what she did was for one reason only – revenge! And there are fewer still that maintain her complete innocence.

For whatever reason, Chloe put a small amount of poison into a birthday cake that was made in honor of the Woodruff's oldest daughter. In with the flour and sugar went a handful of crushed oleander flowers. The two children, and Sarah Mathilda, each had slices of the poisoned cake. Woodruff didn't eat any of it. Before the end of the day, all of them were very sick. Chloe patiently attended to their needs, never realizing that she had given them too much poison. In a matter of hours, all three of them were dead.

The other slaves, perhaps afraid that their owner would punish them also, dragged Chloe from her room and hanged her from a nearby tree. Her body was later cut down, weighted with rocks and thrown into the Mississippi River. Woodruff closed off the children's dining room, where the party was held, and never allowed it to be used again as long as he lived.

Judge Woodruff became disenchanted with his existence and planted Crepe Myrtles as a living memorial for his wife and daughters and then sold the plantation. Tragically, his life was cut short a few years later by a murderer. To this day, the room where the children were poisoned has never again been used for dining. It is now called the game room.

Since her death, the ghost of Chloe has been reported at the Myrtles and was even accidentally photographed by a past owner. The plantation still sells picture postcards today with the cloudy image of what is purported to be Chloe standing between two of the buildings. The former slave is thought to be the most frequently encountered ghost at the Myrtles. She has often been seen in her green turban, wandering the place at night. Sometimes the cries of little children accompany her appearances and at other times, those who are sleeping are startled awake by her face, peering at them from the side of the bed.

Taking into account Jayson's experience and the history of the plantation, I immediately made reservations for the next day.

*\*\*\**

The bark of the live oak tree was deeply grooved as that of the wrinkly skin of an old man. The furrows suggested an age and wisdom that commanded attention, and yet without close examination the detail could be overlooked – ignored as if passing a slow-moving old timer on any given street. The surface of the bark was labyrinthine; a complex maze of channels that guided one's imagination as if that of one's finger tracing paths that lead to nowhere. And it eerily reminded me of the convoluted surface of a brain. What knowledge lay hidden in its undulations, and where would its path lead? This rough three dimensional covering that protects the cambium – the thin and delicate part of the tree that creates the stuff of a tree – possessed an additional eminence; an aspect of time. Unable to completely wrap my arms around its trunk, the size then became a dimensional analysis for time; time that was needed to produce a life form that had witnessed many events at this plantation.

There are dozens of ancient live oaks that stand as both a testament of time and a buffer against intrusion. And as if to consciously perpetuate their legacy, the oversized limbs succumb to gravity producing tortuous extensions that bend to the ground to produce seedlings. And it is from these seedlings, giants will come forth, in their time, to stand as sentinels. The network of giant oaks that stoically go about their business guarantees their continued survival. And as grand as their existence may be, garbed with a draping of Spanish moss, their importance fades to a much lesser tree. One whose presence is underwhelming to that of the oaks, but one whose legacy has its roots planted in a tale of tragedy and death.

I arrived on an April afternoon at the Myrtles Plantation. Attending a conference in Jackson, Mississippi, the drive to St. Francisville, Louisiana via the Natchez Trace Parkway was scenic and rural. The delta farmland still had vestiges of a bygone era, a time when simple lifestyles were bookended with prosperity and poverty – prosperity with regard to wealth and poverty with regard to options. One who was not prosperous was either too poor to exercise any elevated desires in living, or was without civil right to even make the attempt.

The path that led me to the plantation was my recent interest in gaining an understanding of the paranormal. The death of my mother at the hands of a rogue surgeon and the quest for accountability opened the doors of my once closed mind. A mind that was once exposed to things spiritual but had become calloused over time, longed for a revival of hope. Hope that there was more to existing than living this life. And this would be my first field trip to understanding.

The date of this experience was April 2, the first full moon of spring. The Christians used this lunar sign as a time for planting, renewal and forgiveness – a new beginning. The name for the first full moon of spring is the Egg Moon. And my new beginning, my next quest, a higher calling for a deeper understanding of my place in creation, began with a stunning paranormal experience at 3:00 AM in the Judge Clark Woodruff suite at the Myrtles.

Dining at the restaurant at the Myrtles, I met a couple from Monroe, Louisiana. They were staying at an inn several miles away. The Slavant's were interested in the history as they had heard stories since childhood regarding the eerie happenings at the plantation. We sat at the bar at Varnedoe's sipping Sambuca in the tradition of the Italian Underground of World War II; three coffee beans to signal one's membership in that clandestine group. I then invited the couple to visit my room, the Judge Woodruff suite, and it was there we began a conversation that would have a lasting effect on each of those that witnessed the unbelievable.

Placing chairs to form a circle, we began to share stories of the plantation. I told them of my recent research regarding the story of Chloe and the murdered children. Both seemed eager as each leaned forward to hear my whisper. I paused at that part of the tale where the children had succumbed to the poisoning to gather my thoughts, and it was then the unexpected happened. A cry; a child's cry was clearly heard by the Slavant's and myself. We nervously looked at each other and I asked them to point toward the origin of the sound. Each person, beginning with Ms. Slavant, pointed toward the center of our circle, not toward the window, not toward the door – but eyelevel at the epicenter of our gathering.

The downstairs suite was vacant and there were no children on the premises. Ms. Slavant began to noticeably shake, and then began to cry. She then made a hurried exit from the mansion. Mr. Slavant was energized by the experience and wanted to hear more. We continued to talk about Civil War soldiers that hid in walls of the home and their death at the Myrtles. And it was then the deadbolt on the suite locked without assistance from Mr. Slavant or me, or anyone visible. He became uncomfortable and realized we were not alone. He, too, decided to make his departure to check on his wife. I placed a silver coin into a small opening of the trim work of the suite door, a symbolic gesture of thanks and wellbeing.

The traditional view of ghosts is that they are the spirits of dead people that for some reason are *stuck* between this plane of existence and the next, often as a result of some tragedy or trauma. Many ghost hunters and psychics believe that such earthbound spirits don't know they are dead. Veteran ghost hunter Hans Holzer says:

> *A ghost is a human being who has passed out of the physical body, usually in a traumatic state and is not aware usually of his true condition. We are all spirits encased in a physical body. At the time of passing, our spirit body continues into the next dimension. A ghost, on the other hand, due to trauma, is stuck in our physical world and needs to be released to go on.*

There are those that suggest ghosts exist in a kind of limbo in which they haunt the scenes of their deaths, or locations that were pleasant to them in life. Very often, these types of ghosts are able to interact with the living. They are, on some level, aware of the living and react to being seen on the occasions when they materialize. Some psychics are able to communicate with them. And when they do, they often try to help these spirits to understand that they are dead and to move on to the next stage of their existence.

I have returned many times to the Myrtles. And each time I have experienced oddities that would certainly be classified as paranormal. And for some unexplained reason, I disagree with the experts regarding spirits being stuck, or earthbound, as some would say. I have never felt fear as a result of my experiences. Nor, have I felt the need for sympathy for these entities. I simply see, hear, feel and sense those that are free to come and go as they please.

# LILLY'S TOUCH

*There is no logical way to the discovery of these elemental laws.*
*There is only the way of intuition,*
*which is helped by a feeling for the order*
*lying behind the appearance.*
Albert Einstein

The events at the Myrtles, however, pale in significance and magnitude to the happenings at a western Minnesota bed and breakfast known for its physic phenomena. Thayer's Historic Bed and Breakfast in Annandale is an old railroad hotel. Thayer's Hotel was built in 1895, as a railroad hotel using funding from the Soo Line Railroad, by Gus and Caroline Thayer. It was placed on the National Register of Historic Places in 1976. It's been a haunted hotel for a very long time.

The first time Sharon Gammell walked into this building in early 1993, she knew she had to have it. The place was a mess; the porches were in need of some major repairs, plus the faded pink paint was peeling. The inside spaces were dark, dusty, dirty grey, dingy green and orange and everything was covered with an unhappy, dreary, pallor. It was clear that Thayer's Hotel was not being loved at all. Sharon knew she was drawn to this building for a reason and that was to change all that – it was time for an intervention! Thayer's was the place she been talking about and looking for, for some time.

Maybe it was the vision of the *working girls* playfully leaning over the railings of Thayer's *Old West* porches on the front of the building. Maybe it was their call of "Hey! You wanna have some fun?" that she heard. Maybe it was that she knew Thayer's could once more be the beauty it was meant to be and wanted to be a part of it. Maybe it was the way she saw this gorgeous, haunted hotel loved and healthy, again. Maybe, it was all of that and more!

So, in the spring of 1993, Thayer's Hotel stopped operating as a hotel and bar and became Thayer's Historic Bed and Breakfast. The project of restoring was arduous. Commuting from Minneapolis to Annandale, which is over a one hundred-mile round trip, six times per week, the project began with cleaning and painting the inside and outside, hanging wall paper, designing and sewing, moving furniture, and hours and hours of details too numerous to list.

In 1996, Sharon's husband, Warren, was killed when another car drove head on into his; the pain of his death tested her mettle. This created some questions in her resolve as to whether, or not, to complete the project. Her options were to dig in and finish, or quit and return to Minneapolis.

She decided to stay and finish. Today, Thayer's is her home and what a beautiful, well loved, bright, cherry, finely appointed, home and award winning Bed and Breakfast it is! Thayer's has turned out to be every bit what she had imagined it could be, and much more. And, the more, is the intrigue of the grand, old structure.

Thayer's is haunted! Sharon knew that the hotel was haunted, the very first day she walked in. Her husband Warren, Gus Thayer and his wife Caroline Thayer and *the girls* visit regularly, as do many of their friends and customers; plus, the hotel has a few ghostkitties and a ghost-mouse that stop in often. Sharon emphasizes that the ghost are free to come and go.

Thayer's is not an ordinary award winning bed and breakfast; first, it is haunted. And then, by offering customized retreats, workshops and classes in psychic awareness development and paranormal study, ghost hunting packages, plus holiday teas, weddings, and award winning interactive murder mystery dinners that makes Thayer's Historic Bed and Breakfast stand alone as an experience, not just a place to spend a night!

The building pales in significance, however, when its features and history are compare to the innkeeper's talents and gifts. Sharon is an internationally renowned physic. She takes her work seriously. Providing a client with insight and a new look at some old patterns is the stuff that she finds rewarding. Looking into options, talking to friends and pets on the other side, or offering a different view of issues on this side, is helpful and heartwarming, as well as uplifting for her and those she assists.

The word *psychic* originates from the Greek word Psyche meaning the human soul, spirit, or mind. A true Psychic is extremely sensitive. Sensitive to touch, to light, to sounds, to smells, to colors, to energy. According to Sigmund Freud, there are three parts of each human; the ego, the super ego and the id. They relate to how we see ourselves; how others see us, and who we really are. The *who we really are* is the spiritual side of us; the soul; that part of us that is made in the image of God.

It is the soul that psychics look into to view the past, the present, and the future for their patrons. Each of us has the mental side, the physical and the spiritual side. Thus each of us has psychic abilities. When the phone rings and you know who it is; you have a dream that becomes a reality; you know you are going to see or hear from a person; you have a *gut* feeling that something is going to happen; or you say the same thing at the same time as someone else. These are all examples of psychic abilities. It is just that there are some who have developed and fine tuned that ability. And there are others who did not have to develop and fine tune; it was always there; as with Sharon.

To develop psychic abilities one must be sensitive to vibrations of thought, sound, ideas or images appearing or floating around in one's head. One must be sensitive to others. To be sensitive as to how others think, feel, act, and re-act and sensitive to other's needs, wants and desires, and to all new ideas that come flooding into your mind.

A psychic must have an expanded awareness, *seeing* what is not obvious to the physical senses or logical mind. Because psychic ability does not operate in the usual realm of time or space, it may be possible to tune into past events, or future trends, as well as loved ones at a distance. Additionally, hidden causes and potentials may be accessed. Psychic ability is what we often refer to as the sixth sense.

In a psychic reading Sharon does not tell one how to live their life; she does offer suggestions on how to make life work in a way that is fulfilling and rewarding. When she makes a prediction during a reading, that is what it is – a prediction. If one does not like the prediction, one can change what one is doing and change the future outcome!

***

I had flown into Minneapolis and negotiated the wind and snow for what would have normally been a one hour drive that took more than two hours to navigate. The temperature was expected to reach a low of minus 26 degrees Fahrenheit that night. The structure was a dominate landmark as its image became clearer through the veil of windblown snow. The structure resembled a large sugar cube, coated with snow it was completely square with equal height, width and depth. The front of the three story structure was adorned with wooden railings that bordered a balcony at each level. I checked into the bed and breakfast on a cold February evening, a night that would prove to be intriguing, to say the least.

Those that stay at the inn are fully aware that Sharon is a well-known physic. She schedules classes on selected dates each year to train those interested in discovering the traits and practices of spirits and ghosts. Tonight, her home was occupied by twelve guests, all who have a desire to experience an encounter with the unknown, or at least the forgotten.

Dinner was prepared by the innkeeper. Chef Sharon once owned and operated restaurants in Minneapolis and St. Paul, establishments that catered to the savviest of diners. The guests did not have an option regarding the cuisine, the selection had been made by the chef and the Osso Bucco was presented by the assistant. Dessert followed dinner and then, an after dinner drink of coffee was presented and the stage was set for a once in a lifetime experience.

Sharon took a position next to the fireplace and began a discussion about spirits, ghosts, spirit guides and guardian angels. Everyone was on the edge of their seats. Questions were asked and the responses were elegant and simple; answers that made one think, why I didn't think of that. A common theme of the questions focused either on the strange occurrences at the bed and breakfast, or if one's home can also be haunted. Sharon explained that most of what is dismissed as an unexplained occurrence such as the finding a lost article that one has searched for only to find it in plain sight, is often a bizarre experience. And the occasional sound of unexplained footsteps, the scent of a strange fragrance, or the slamming of doors are happenings most everyone has experienced. Yet, some are still somewhat skeptical and dismiss the events as incidental. One is either unable, or willing to accept the signs of a haunting, or they are open and intrigued.

A mistake that is commonly made is to compare a real paranormal event with a Hollywood production. Even though it may seem strange to comprehend, ghosts may appear to be shy and low keyed. This may be an accurate representation of their personality, or it may be a lack of energy to become fully manifested as they wish. Some ghosts may be stuck in what we call a habit. Perhaps the slamming of a door is the singular action in which they want to be recognized. Or, maybe a variety of phenomena is best suited for the more aggressive. All in all, strange things happen and the strangest and rarest is a full body apparition. The key to experiencing a paranormal event is recognizing it when it occurs. There are several phenomena that are indicative of a paranormal event.

Unexplained noises are the most common. Footsteps, banging, scratching; all are characteristics of *someone* that wants to be heard. And depending on the personality of the ghost, the sounds can be subtle, or loud. Hearing sounds is an experience that one has as the paranormal event occurs; other happenings are experienced after the fact. Such as with doors and windows that were securely fastened that later are found to be open. And a common and yet overlooked occurrence is the movement of objects as if something is playing hide-and-seek with one's belongings. How many times has one said to one's self, I don't remember leaving this here, or there? And stranger still is the catching from the corner of one's eye a shape, or shadow as it moves from view. Animals often see these entities and the occurrence creates a predictable reaction; barking from a dog, a bowed back and hissing from a cat or the refusal by either to enter a room. These are a few examples of what we attempt to explain away as the creaking of an old house, the forgetfulness of a tired human, the overactive imagination of the mind, or a nervous pet. And yet, there are times when one knows without a doubt, one is being watched.

Stronger evidence for a haunting includes much of what has been mentioned with an added caveat; actually seeing or feeling an event as it occurs, or seeing the source of the event. Seeing a door open, witnessing the moving of a book, experiencing electronic appliances turn on and off, or feeling a touch by an unseen hand are psychokinetic phenomena. Cries, whispers and music are sounds that are quite different from the sound of a slamming door and indicate a much stronger presence. These occurrences are characteristic of an elevated experience in the paranormal.

Rarer still, are what is categorized as poltergeist phenomenon. Objects such as furniture levitating, pictures flying from the walls or doors slamming with great force are signs of what one could interpret as mal-intent. The appearance of writings or symbols on the walls, floor or ceiling, as well as on one's body and footprints are profound. Physical assaults that include slapping, scratching and being tossed about have been documented. Albeit, these occurrences are rare, these are what most Westerners identify as the presence of ghosts and a haunting.

The question and answer session concluded. Then Sharon gave each student an assignment, the task of exploring the inn and recording each and every thought, sensation, sound and sight that is experienced. Equipped with an extensive crash-course in Ghost Hunting 101, I started on the third floor to separate myself from the pack and entered room number 304. The room was cold despite the efforts of plastic sheathing on the windows to hold back the draft. Remembering the instruction that was given by Sharon,

I walked into the room and opened my senses for whatever might be received. The process was a strange contradiction, one where each sense was to be heightened to not miss any stimuli, and the next to not create false readings of an uncontrolled imagination. The admonishment was to be true to one's self.

Leaning against the bedpost, I remained motionless moving only my eyes to catch any visual occurrence. It was then I felt something brush my shoulder; contact that had the intensity of a baby's touch. And at that same moment a thought came into my mind, one that was clear as a bell, it was as though someone whispered it into my ear. I heard the name with my ears, or my mind, or some other mode of knowing of which I was not yet aware, John. John. I did not know anyone named John. I chronicled my experience and moved to the next room.

On the second floor, in room 206, a sensation of a familiar smell was overwhelming. Although the home is a smoke free establishment, the aroma of pipe smoke was prevalent. I took an additional step into the room and the smell disappeared. I then stepped back to the original position where I smelled the pipe smoke and the aroma returned. Only in that specific place, an area the size of a serving tray, did I experience that scent.

I returned to the hallway and took a seat near the top of the stairs to record my experience. Taking my work seriously, and with care to be accurate and precise, I found myself being annoyed by a cat. The cat was doing what cats do, rubbing its body about my feet and legs. I leaned without looking to brush the cat away. The rubbing continued. When I looked to see which cat was disturbing me, Mr. Tennessee, Miss Sadie or Sam-Sam, nothing was there. The rubbing continued with no visible signs of a cat. Even though this would have frightened me in any other venue, it did not cause any fear in me. I continued to record that encounter as the rubbing continued, and then I returned to the dining area for the next phase of training.

Each guest was tasked with doing what I had done, and then Sharon asked each to share their experience. I began with the aroma in room 207. She interrupted and asked if I experienced the aroma of pipe smoke, and of course that was what was experienced. I then told of my experience in 303, and quickly said that something touched me on my right shoulder. She then said that was John and he likes to whisper in one's ear. I then mentioned the rubbing of my legs by an unseen cat; she said the cat's name is Professor Herald Squeak.

The group looked to me for validation. With a dazed countenance I held my writing pad so that all could see my notes. The document described a feeling of something touching me and whispering in my ear the name, John. The documentation listed the smell of a pipe smoker. Each guest leaned to get a better view of my writing pad and then of me, I felt as though I was the event. The remaining guest had similar tales, equally compelling and bizarre.

The focus then shifted on improving our ability to sense the unseen by controlling the energy field that surrounds a person. Sharon asked for a volunteer and I made myself available. She placed me in front of the fireplace and asked me to close my eyes. She then positioned herself behind me; I learned later that the distance was ten feet. She then asked me to tell her when I felt her touch. I stood quietly, waiting for the touch and then it happened; a slight push. One that caused me to slightly lose my balance and as I turned to comment, Sharon was still five feet from me. I had felt her touch without having her physically touching me. I observed as each participant took an opportunity to experience this remote touching. All were taken aback with having the same experience.

And what happened next, as if enough had not happened already was truly remarkable. Sharon placed me in front of the fire place and instructed me to request a touch from Lilly. Lilly is a resident of the home, one of the invisible occupants. She made herself known to Sharon when a portrait was found by a staff member. Lilly's profession, among the living, was what most would consider a healer and a midwife. And with Sharon's intuitiveness and with Lilly's energy, she became a part of the experience at Thayers. And Emily assists with the Ghost 101 classes conducted by the host.

I felt a bit self conscious. I sensed I could trust Sharon and yet the Western influence of discarding the paranormal as that which was limited to the black arts was overbearing. Yet, I tried to comply by letting go, letting go of expectation and ego and letting happen what may. Closing my eyes, I asked Lilly to touch my shoulder. After a couple of requests and a moment of silence I felt a slight, yet distinct nudge on my shoulder; a nudge that caused my shoulder to dip noticeably to the amazement of the guests. Each attendee had an opportunity to interact with the paranormal, to experience the touch of the unseen.

The evening had been eye-opening at the very least. The exercise in developing a better sensitivity to one's surroundings was extremely beneficial, having had a happening with regard to what most would term a paranormal event was exhilarating. The titles of ghost and spirit are often used interchangeably by most people with each hinting a predisposition toward being either malevolent or benevolent. This former railroad hotel, however, is not frightening. It does not make one feel threatened. Nor does it have a dark and sorted history. Other than a few industrious ladies trying to make a living in the distant past, nothing criminal occurred within is walls.

As if that were not enough, the next morning Sharon conducted a psychic *reading* for me. A room adjacent to the front parlor was the site for this intimate setting. The room is such that when one is there, there are hundreds of objects of various sizes, colors and shapes to capture one's attention and imagination. And as strange as it may seem, when one leaves the room that detail escapes the memory and all one remembers are the participants, the cards and the table. It is as if the focus narrows in respect to the center of the room so that one's life can, in turn, open in every respect.

Sharon placed before me three decks of cards. I selected the more worn deck. She then began to display the cards in a geometric pattern, stopping periodically to offer comments. Her observations were about the past, present and future. Some were easy for me to interpret as in the case of health issues not previously known by Sharon. And some that were not so easy to interpret such as past lives and future events.

She placed a few cards on the table and said that I have lived six previous lives. And in one of those lives I was a leader, a person that was in charge of the well-being of a large group of people. And that I had acted irresponsibly and that had caused extreme hardship regarding adequate food supplies. And for that reason I have had for several years the overwhelming desire to hoard and store food for what I expect to be a time in the future of want and need. And that was exactly my mindset. I had spent a great deal of time prior to my visit researching the shelf life of canned goods and dried goods, and how to purify water. That planning had as its source an over whelming sense of urgency for what the future held and for the basics of life. That was a side of me I had not shared with anyone, and she knew.

Sharon continued placing cards on the table and said you, or someone close to you would visit Greece within the next few months. My son spent a week in Greece that summer with the Latin club; the trip had already been planned at the time of the reading.

Additional cards were placed on the table and she then said that a relative of mine would be offered early retirement the following summer. The relative received that offer the next winter, although it was summer time in South America where the offer was presented.

Many other comments were made. Some were inconsequential, and a few were extremely noteworthy. One proved to be tale telling with regard to the intense nature of the prediction. The placement of a card caused Sharon to sit back in her seat. Her mannerisms are professional and her body language is always guarded. Her demeanor is that of an advocate for her clients. At that moment, however, she let her guard down and made a stunning prediction. She described a worksite of a sibling, an industrial scene where gray piping and metal platform were in place. And she then described a red object affecting the site and the platform resulting in as many as three deaths. My sibling would not be harmed.

Nine months later I received a call from my sister cancelling holiday travel plans because of an accident. An accident at a job site for which she was managing that resulted in two deaths and the permanent disability of the third. Gray piping that contained a red pressure valve exploded causing the fatal injuries. The worst accident prior to this experience in twenty five years was nothing more severe than a broken bone.

All in all, the happenings at Thayer's Bed and Breakfast and the exposure to Sharon Gammell's intuitive insight are by far the most intense experience to date. And to expect more may sound a bit greedy. But more is what I have received. She has served as a mentor and life-coach in preparing me for future endeavors that, yes she predicted, I would be successful in pursuing.

# NO BRAKES

*Angele Dei,*
*qui custos es mei,*
*me, tibi commissum pietate superna,*
*illumina, custodi,*
*rege et guberna.*
*Amen.*

It was 3:00 AM on Interstate 20 west of Vicksburg, Mississippi. Crossing the Mississippi River Bridge unnerved me, particularly at night. The annoying hum of the tires interacting with the steel-grated crossing, and the apprehension that the structure supporting me was well over 60 feet above the water terrified me. The only comfort for the two mile span was the cloudless night and bright moon that guided me. That made the drive a bit more tolerable.

The trees along the river bank were illuminated with a silvery light that cast shadows, creating two dimensional silhouettes. Dimming the dashboard lights to improve my view, depth of field was lost as shadow and light played games with my vision. The boundary separating light from shadow was wispy and unclear, creating the illusion of movement, as if the trees were shifting from their rooted nest.

The satellite radio was tuned to Coast To Coast AM and George Noory's guest was intriguing as usual. The subject of tonight's show focused on the spiritual realm; spirit guides and guardian angels. Each caller to the show had a specific question that was preceded by one's own tale of the unusual. Some of the tales were more believable than were others. And if I were to call I would most likely skip the story and proceed to the question, I had no tale to tell.

Sipping a cup of truck-stop coffee that was brewed with a driver's intent in mind, it provided a much needed stimulant to stay awake. My journey tonight was the result of a late-night phone call at 11:00 PM from the Vice President of Production regarding an emergency meeting. The meeting had been hastily scheduled to be held at the branch office in Shreveport, Louisiana at 8:00 AM the following morning. It was too late to arrange a flight, and the drive from Jackson, Mississippi was uneventful and easy. I suppose most people would have opted out of the required engagement with a myriad of reasons to do so. My parents, on the other hand, had instilled in me an unyielding work ethic. As a school child if I were sick, my Dad would encourage me to go to school. Insisting that I was going to be sick anyway, so why not be productive while being sick. So, in good conscience, I could not decline the request.

West of the bridge I saw a hitchhiker. She was alone and desperately waving her arms above her head for someone to stop. I did not see a car, nor had I noticed one disabled in my travel, and my first thought was why she is alone and how did she get here. I looked in the rearview mirror to begin my exit from the highway. As I placed my foot on the brake pedal to stop, the pedal offered no resistance and my foot rested on the floor of the car. No brakes! I began to pump the brake pedal, slowly at first, and then with added concern. Certainly, I could coast to a stop but not in time to assist the hitchhiker. In fact, I dismissed the possibility of offering her aid and drove slowly to the next exit with plans to use the emergency brake as an alternative.

Approaching exit Number 171, the Tallulah exit, I once again tried to apply my brakes and with different results. The brakes worked perfectly. I stopped to refill my coffee and continued west toward Shreveport. I changed the radio setting to a local channel as I drew nearer to my destination. The news bulletin sent a chill throughout my spine. Two carjacking victims were found east of Tallulah on Interstate 20. One was dead, two gunshots to the head, and the other was wounded and left dying. The wounded victim gave an account of the crime, an account that described an attractive woman hitchhiking. And when they stopped to offer assistance, the woman jumped into the back seat of the car and held their attention by removing her blouse. With their attention focused on the woman's breasts, a man armed with a handgun ran from the wooded area near the highway and attacked the two men. Shooting both and dragging them from the car.

At the time I felt fortunate that I could not stop and certainly I would have been a victim if I had. The next day, I had the braking system checked and the mechanic found nothing faulty. The strange coincidence of a failed braking system and the inability to stop saved my life. At the time I considered the series of events to be a stroke of good luck.

A few months later, I was on temporary assignment in Alexandria, Louisiana. My apartment was a converted home that was well over 100 years old. The owner was a local entrepreneur that supplemented her income with rental properties. This piece of property had been subdivided into three apartments. This triplex was located in the historic part of town near the intersections of Jackson and Chester. The reconstruction of the home was performed in a manner to preserve the image and style of the 1930s.

Unit number one was assigned to me and the dwelling had both a front and rear entrance. The front lawn bordered Jackson Street, a busy thoroughfare that did not provide street parking. The alternative was the alley. Although narrow and cluttered with an assortment of discarded items, it did provide a way to access the rear door of the residence. The developer had meticulously carved out an area to park a car that seemed as much an oasis amid the disorder as a simple parking spot.

The designated area was separated from the rear yard by a wrought iron fence. It was a fence that had a distinctive characteristic ornamental look with an interesting caveat; it was adorned with a unique feature that I had seen on a recent trip to the French Quarter. Small iron features of the fence were fashioned as ears of corn and painted yellow. Beyond the fence was a yard, a courtyard that was busy with plantings and statues. The theme of the landscaping was a blending of a flea market, a museum and a cemetery. It was a peculiar mixture of bad taste and gaudiness. The walkway from my car to the backdoor was anything but a direct path, much like a roped aisle one would negotiate at airport security.

My responsibilities required me to entertain clients with dinner presentations; presentations that were intended to reinforce the company's core values and to supply a continuous flow of adult beverage. These events were considered a necessary consequence of conducting business and were often brief in duration and somewhat tiresome. However, one dinner presentation that was scheduled on an October evening was atypical, that night happened to be the birthday of a colleague. The opportunity to consume free drinks and a reason to escalate that consumption made for a long evening as I stroked the egos of those who put bread on my table. People that I barely knew were wishing my colleague a happy birthday with slurred speech and with gin-like halitosis.

Signaling the bartender to wrap things up, I instructed the hostess to hail a couple of cabs to transport the impaired to their hotels. Hand shaking and last minute jocularity tried my nerves as I pushed the more obnoxious from the restaurant to the sidewalk. Settling the $1,200.00 tab and dropping a couple of Ben Franklins to the selected members of the wait staff, I made my exit from The Port of Call lounge and to my temporary home. The clock at Hibernian Bank read 1:00 AM.

The drive from the lounge to my Jackson Street destination was less than five minutes. I was the only car on the street except for that of a city policeman who flashed his blue lights as if to provide a warning that he was watching me. And to fulfill his need for authority, I slowed my speed and complied with every detail of the law. My evening had been one of extreme accommodation to my clients, which in itself is exhausting. And then the abject capitulation to this authority figure raised within me a defiant passion.

I turned onto the alley leading to the rear parking of my apartment. Parking the car in my assigned slot, I retrieved my briefcase from the trunk and took two steps toward the gate leading to courtyard and the pathway to the dwelling. Something overcame me. I did not see anything unusual, nor did I hear or smell anything that should have caused me alarm. I simply was possessed with an overwhelming since of terror, one that caused me to experience shortness of breath and one that caused me to sweat. My heart raced and something within me said to leave. I paused and then heard an audible directive, now!

I hurried to the car and tossed the briefcase onto the passenger seat. Putting the car in reverse, I flung pea gravel of the parking pad onto the courtyard and then changing to drive I sped toward Chester Street and away from my fear. Stopping at the convenience store to regain my composure, I saw the same city cop that had flashed the blue lights of his squad car at me earlier. I was tempted to discuss my experience with him, but what experience did I have. I then decided to return and break with the rules of the landlord and park on the sidewalk on Jackson Street. I hurried to the front door and to the presumed safety of my home.

I did not sleep well that night; in fact I slept on the sofa with the aid of late night television. The light of morning brought a deep sigh of relief as I dismissed the frightening events as an imagination out of control. Removing the Community Coffee tin from the shelf, I began my daily routine of brewing a pot of poor-man's Prozac and I then walked to the back door, my intended point of entry the previous night, and opened it. It was then my fear was resurrected.

To my panic, on the landing at my rear door, was a pile of cigarette butts, more than two dozen. I did not place them there and the residents of the other apartments did not smoke. Someone had been there, sitting on the step of the landing, waiting for me to return. My confusion was twofold, why would someone wait for me and what did I sense and what did I experience that caused me to fear for my life – why did I have the experience? On two occasions, months apart, circumstances and intuitiveness most likely had saved my life, or at the very least from harm. And my interest in what, or who, assisted me became an obsession.

*** 

Those that claim to have seen a Guardian Angel describe them as youthful, strong, radiant and magnificent. Light often accompanies them and one feels profoundly reverent in their presence. These characteristics notwithstanding, Guardian Angels have the ability to change shapes and to conform to the environment and situation. The general conception of a blue-eyed, blonde-haired winged protector from God is flawed. Their command of nature permits them to manipulate the supposedly immutable laws of physics to create what they will, and to appear as they wish; often as pure light, or as a disembodied voice.

In independent studies, over eighty percent of Westerners believe in the existence of theses divine protectors. Half of all Americans believe an Angel is assigned to them specifically. And one third of that same polled group has felt the presence or influence of theses beings in their lives. Some believe that the Angels are departed loved ones rather than spiritual beings created specifically to watch over creation.

Records dating back over 3,000 years to the time of Ancient Egypt and Mesopotamia chronicles the belief in a structured order of supernatural beings that served as managers of all aspects of nature. There was also a belief in a set of counterparts to these benevolent protectors, those equal but opposite entities that ruled the underworld and was the source of ill fate for humankind. All religions promote a model of the existence of Guardian Angels. In the Sanskrit text of the Vedas, *angira* is the word for angel. In Hebrew it is either *malakh*, meaning *messenger*, or *bene elohim*, meaning God's children. In Arabic the name is *malakah* similar to the Hebrew name.

Stories of Guardian Angels have a number of consistencies. One is that they are considered to be paraphysical. That is to say, they can appear from nothing and form as solid matter and disappear similarly. The activities of these protectors are chronicled in the Old and New Testaments. Appearing out of the blue to rescue prophets from a fiery furnace, wrestling with stubborn men, and providing general support as experienced by Jesus himself as he was fed and protected by the Angels.

There are those that believe that the good among us become angels at the time of death. This is inconsistent with essentially all ancient traditions. The creation of the angels is separate and apart for that of man. And the Bible list a hierarchy placing humankind a *little lower* than the angels.

What is often missed in the understanding of the Guardian Angels is their role in guiding one to a higher spiritual experience. That quiet voice of reason that prompts one to take a path of moderation, or to take chance to consider a new idea is the prompting of one's Protector. The consistency in the Bible is that from the beginning to the end, the presence of spiritual beings is never absent. They, in fact, play a key role in the orchestration of what unfolds. And the Bible does not skirt the issue by making the existence of Angels a dream or a metaphor; it treats them as real as Christ himself.

Islam is similar in that there are three levels of beings. There are the angels which are called *malakah*. These are beings of the highest order, they are beings of light. Then there are the *al-jinn*. These being represent the second order and are multi-dimensional entities. Then there are humans made from the dust of the earth. The *al-jinn* can either assist, or hinder humans in the lives.

The idea of Guardian Angels is often dismissed as the musings of children and their bedtime stories. The concept that there are entities fluttering about to intercede on one's behalf is considered by some childish. And that perception could be easily adopted if it were not for the fact that we are spiritual beings ourselves.

Guardian Angels are spiritual beings that are *assigned* to assist people here on Earth in various ways. Whether there is one angel per person, one angel for several persons or several angels for one person is of little consequence in that they are quite capable of performing their feats. But whether you believe in them or not or whether you want one or not, you do have a Guardian Angel.

Guardian Angels intercept at many junctures in our lives and help wherever they can to make our lives run smoothly. Their intercession can be subtle, or stark. One is often inspired by a thought that spurs them into action. Others experience super-human strength, such as in the case of a woman being able to lift a car long enough to free her trapped child. There are stories similar to a runaway truck, with an unconscious driver at the wheel that inexplicably swerves sharply at the last moment to avoid colliding with a school bus. Luck, coincidence and miracle, have been words used as rationalization for the actions of Guardian Angels who intercede on our behalf.

Angels don't always come to a person's aid every time it's asked for. Sometimes, they stand back so that we can experience life, and while giving loving support, they wait with us. And the times we feel most alone, as it is darkest before the dawn, our answers come with patience and trust. One is never alone.

*Angel of God, my guardian dear*
*to whom God's love commits me here.*
*Ever this day/night be at my side*
*to light, to guard, to rule and guide.*
*Amen*

# IN SHIPS WITHOUT WINGS

*The ship of heaven guides its self and will
not accept a wooden rudder.*
Ralph Waldo Emerson

His weathered face and long white hair lent a surreal credibility to the story, a story that was told to his ancestors over a thousand years ago. The Hopi elder's countenance blended with the rough features of the Painted Desert of northern Arizona. It was as if he and the desert were one, made of the same stuff. The landscape was an enigma, and so was the man. At a glance, the desert was featureless and without color. And when one paused to look more closely at a particular focal point, it was then the detail and color became breathtakingly obvious. And as with the desert landscape, so it was with the elder.

To form a first impression of the sage that was based solely on his presence would be a mistake. One might confuse his ragged jeans and slow speech with poverty and diminished intelligence. Looking deeply into his eyes, however, and listening to his simple wisdom, made one pay close attention to his wealth of insight and heightened sensitivity.

The elder leaned and placed his left forearm on his knee and then took his walking stick and sketched in the sand a crude rendition of a Hopi Petroglyph; The Prophecy Rock. A petroglyph, when interpreted correctly, forewarned the Hopi of coming events that would shape their world. The elder began by drawing a human-like stick figure that held a bowl in its left hand. The figure represented the Great Spirit. And the contents of the bowl were the Great Spirit's directives for the Hopi to lay down their weapons. He looked up and said that battles fought with weapons are lost before being waged.

The elder then drew a vertical line next to the stick figure. The vertical line represented a time scale measured in thousands of years, and the point where the Great Spirit touches the line marks his return to earth. He continued to explain the meaning as he drew two horizontal, parallel lines to the right of the vertical time line that represented different paths of life. The lower line symbolizes the narrow path of continuous life in harmony with nature, a life that the Hopi live. And the upper path represents the wide road of the white man, one built with scientific achievements and materialism.

Four small human stick-figures were drawn on the upper road. The four figures represented, on one level, the past three worlds of the Hopi, and the present. On another level, the figures indicate that some of the Hopi will travel the white man's path, having been seduced by its glamour. These stick figures were drawn with their heads disconnected from the body symbolizing a type of disengagement from the spiritual.

He then drew a vertical line connecting the upper and lower paths. He then placed a cross where the line connected with the Hopi's Path of Life. The crude crucifix marked the arrival of the white man, and his religion into the lives of the Hopi. Next to the cross, he drew two circles on the lower path of Life representing *the great shaking of the earth*; the two World Wars.

The Hopi shield in the lower right corner symbolized the Earth and the Four-Corners area where the Hopi have been preserved. The arms of the cross also represent the four directions in which they migrated according to the instructions of the Great Spirit. And the dots represent the four colors of Hopi corn, and the four racial colors of humanity.

The elder then drew another vertical line connecting the two paths to the right of the circles. He said this marks the last chance for people to return to their roots and revere nature before the great Purification. Beyond this vertical line, the upper road of the white man disintegrates as the elder drew a squiggly line. The lower path of life continued in prosperity as nature supplied corn that was represented by two crudely drawn cornstalks.

The elder then took his walking cane and erased the drawing in the dirt and reclined in his chair. He described the Four Worlds of the Hopi. The first world was Tokpela, the beginning when space was without limit, and time and life did not exist. Taiowa, the creator, formed a helper, Sotuknang, to produce nine universes; one for Taiowa, one for Sotuknang and seven for future use.

Sotuknang created Kokyangwuti, the spider woman, to create humankind. She accomplished this by mixing dirt of varying colors with her saliva to a fashion a male and a female for each of the four races. The elder then leaned over and scooped a handful of dirt as if to demonstrate the process. As he presented his mixture of spit and earth; a part of me expected much more than mud. The old man smiled as if he had performed this act before, to audiences that were much younger.

Kokyangwuti then gave each of the four races a unique language. And the four races lived together in harmony even though they did not talk to each other verbally; they communicated telepathically.

And as if to anticipate my next question, the elder said humans have five vibration centers.

The first is the Kopavi, the open door, which is the soft spot on top of the head. And at this point in creation, the beginning, as with a newborn, this tender area has the ability to receive messages from the creator. The second vibration area is the brain and it permits humans to think for themselves; what you in your religion call freewill. The third vibration area is the throat. It is a place to gather air to sustain the body and produce sound. The fourth vibration area is the heart. It is the physical expression of life itself. And the last vibration area is the navel. It is the seat of the creator and the source of one's gut feelings. With each listing, the old man rubbed that portion of his body. Not so much as a tutorial for me as much as it was reacquainting him with his vibration centers.

Humans were without sickness in the first world of Tokpela until evil arrived. And when one became ill the shaman would lay hands on the vibration areas to monitor the clarity of the body. The medicine man could then determine if the illness was organic or mental; a result of something unseen or of something believed.

He insisted that I look directly into his eyes as he summarized the first world. The name of Tokpela means endless space. The people were in agreement with each other and were comfortable with their place in creation. The direction of this world was west and the color was sikyangpu, yellow and the mineral was sikyasvu, gold.

The second world was called Tokpa. In this world, the people lost their focus regarding their place in creation, and became corrupt. They used their vibration centers for personal gain, and forgot the laws of the spider woman. An entity appeared in the form of a Mochni, a Mockingbird. Lavaihoya taught the people how to talk, and created jealousies within the races and divisions between the races.

In the first world of Tokpela, humans and animals lived together. In the second world the animals separated themselves from humans. The guardian spirit of the animals laid hands on the animals creating a gland that made the animals wild and fearful of man. Katoya, another entity of corruption, came in the form of a snake and escalated jealousy and division to warring.

Sotuknang was then instructed by Taiowa, the Great Spirit, to gather the humans that had resisted corruption so that they may be saved from the destruction of the world. The righteous were instructed to follow their Kopavi, and this would allow them to see a cloud by day and a star by night. The ones who followed their Kopavi, representing all races, gathered at the final destination of *one mind*.

Sotuknang then asked the ant people to house the chosen humans in their ant Kiva. As the surface world was being destroyed by fire, the humans were to learn the industrious habits of the ant people. The ant people's first lesson was that of sharing, the humans did not lack for anything because the ant people rationed their supplies to assure abundance for the guest. And as lessons were taught and learned the surface of the earth was reshaped by volcanism so that no human would recognize any feature. The humans were then instructed to go and multiply and sing praise to Taiowa.

The lessons learned from the ant people were soon corrupted. The industriousness of the ant people became the foundation for greed as the humans produced and bartered for things that were not needed. The practice of hoarding goods and materials produced a desire to have more. And with more possessions, larger cities were built and roads constructed to connect them. Soon arguments and wars based on jealousy of possessions, and fear of lost wealth, caused the wicked to laugh and the pure at heart to sing the praise of Sotuknang.

Sotuknang heard their cry and once again asked the ant people to shelter the righteous. The surface of the earth was once again destroyed. This time the guardians of the poles; the twins, Poqanghoya and Palongawhoya, left their positions and caused the icecaps to melt, the continents to shift, strange weather patterns to develop and the accumulative result was an ice age. The earth's magnetic poles shifted polarity and the world reversed its rotation. And when the twins returned to their polar positions, the earth stabilized and the humans emerged from the ant Kiva with the same instructions to go forth and multiply and sing praises to Taiowa. And the absence of praise would mean corruption exist.

Once again the elder asked that I focus my attention to his eyes. The name of the second world, Tokpa, means dark midnight. The direction of this world was south and the color was blue and the mineral was qochasiva, silver.

The third world of the Hopi was called Kuskurza. In this world humans used sex for personal gain – prostitution. And the lessons learned from the previous two worlds were soon forgotten, and the division between the corrupt and the righteous widened. Advanced cites and politics became commonplace, and pursuit of materialistic gain became the norm. Wars continued based on fear and jealousy and humans built flying machines using animal hides to attack cities.

Sotuknang heard fewer praises and presumed corruption. Sotuknang communicated to the pure at heart to hide in cut reeds with hurusuki – cornmeal – to protect and sustain them. Sotuknang then destroyed the surface of the earth with floodwaters. Spider woman called the humans from the reeds with their cornmeal which had not diminished even though it had been consumed. The people sent birds to look for land and finding a number of small islands as temporary homes. They then came to a larger portion of land that would provide a migratory route for the journey to the Hotevilla. Before departing on their migration, Sotuknang pointed to the islands that had provided temporary homes as they sank beneath the sea. Just as footsteps wash away so, too, do the islands of your journey.

The fourth world is called Tuwaqachi, which means World Complete. This world is less desirable than the previous because of the extremes. Hot and cold, green and barren, wet and dry, these variations of climate made life more difficult and unpredictable.

Massaw was assigned as the caretaker of the fourth world. He had been admonished in the third world for an indiscretion and was later forgiven and granted eternal life in Tuwaqachi. Massaw told the people that Taiowa had given them a Road Plan, and they knew what to do. The direction of the fourth world is north and the color is white. The Road Plan is described as the Prophecy Rock, the drawing of the Hopi Petroglyph the elder had created in the sand.

The elder paused and I asked if he could discuss the prophecies of the Hopi. He smiled as if to encourage me to be patient. He then said that Massaw instructed the Hopi to settle in what is now called the Four Corners area of Northeast Arizona on the third mesa. The original settlement was founded in 1100AD and named Oraibi. There was a division amongst the Hopi in 1906 that forced the Traditionalist to create a new settlement called Hotevilla. Those that hold to the Hopi belief accept the premise that what happens in Hotevilla happens to the world. Or better said Hotevilla is the seat of the planet's soul. He then placed in my hand a worn and torn folded piece of paper and it chronicled a strange tale.

The following is an extraordinary Hopi prophecy that was first published in a mimeographed manuscript that circulated among several Methodist and Presbyterian churches in 1959. Some of the prophecies were published in 1963 by Frank Waters in The Book of the Hopi. The account begins by describing how, while driving along a desert highway one hot day in the summer of 1958, a minister named David Young stopped to offer a ride to an Indian elder, who accepted with a nod. After riding in silence for several minutes, the Indian said:

*I am White Feather, a Hopi of the ancient Bear Clan. In my long life I have traveled through this land, seeking out my brothers, and learning from them many things full of wisdom. I have followed the sacred paths of my people, who inhabit the forests and many lakes in the east, the land of ice and long nights in the north, and the places of holy altars of stone built many years ago by my brothers' fathers in the south. From all these I have heard the stories of the past, and the prophecies of the future. Today, many of the prophecies have turned to stories, and few are left – the past grows longer, and the future grows shorter.*

*And now White Feather is dying. His sons have all joined his ancestors, and soon he too shall be with them. But there is no one left, no one to recite and pass on the ancient wisdom. My people have tired of the old ways – the great ceremonies that tell of our origins, of our emergence into the Fourth World, are almost all abandoned, forgotten, yet even this has been foretold. The time grows short.*

*My people await Pahana, the lost White Brother, from the stars as do all our brothers in the land. He will not be like the white men we know now, who are cruel and greedy. We were told of their coming long ago. But still we await Pahana.*

*He will bring with him the symbols, and the missing piece of that sacred tablet now kept by the elders, given to him when he left, that shall identify him as our True White Brother.*

*The Fourth World shall end soon, and the Fifth World will begin. This the elders everywhere know. The Signs over many years have been fulfilled, and so few are left.*

*This is the First Sign: We are told of the coming of the white-skinned men, like Pahana, but not living like Pahana men who took the land that was not theirs. And men who struck their enemies with thunder.*

*This is the Second Sign: Our lands will see the coming of spinning wheels filled with voices. In his youth, my father saw this prophecy come true with his eyes – the white men bringing their families in wagons across the prairies.*

*This is the Third Sign: A strange beast like a buffalo but with great long horns will overrun the land in large numbers. These White Feather saw with his eyes – the coming of the white men's cattle.*

*This is the Fourth Sign: The land will be crossed by snakes of iron.*

*This is the Fifth Sign: The land shall be crisscrossed by a giant spider's web.*

*This is the Sixth sign: The land shall be crisscrossed with rivers of stone that make pictures in the sun.*

*This is the Seventh Sign: You will hear of the sea turning black, and many living things dying because of it.*

*This is the Eight Sign: You will see many youth, who wear their hair long like my people, come and join the tribal nations, to learn their ways and wisdom.*

*And this is the Ninth and Last Sign: You will hear of a dwelling-place in the heavens, above the earth, that shall fall with a great crash. It will appear as a blue star. Very soon after this, the ceremonies of my people will cease.*

*These are the Signs that great destruction is coming. The world shall rock to and fro. The white man will battle against other people in other lands; with those who possessed the first light of wisdom. There will be many columns of smoke and fire such as White Feather has seen the white man make in the deserts not far from here. Only those which come will cause disease and a great dying. Many of my people, understanding the prophecies, shall be safe. Those who stay and live in the places of my people also shall be safe. Then there will be much to rebuild. And soon – very soon afterward – Pahana will return. He shall bring with him the dawn of the Fifth World. He shall plant the seeds of his wisdom in their hearts. Even now the seeds are being planted. These shall smooth the way to the Emergence into the Fifth World.*

*But White Feather shall not see it. I am old and dying. You perhaps will see it; in time, in time...*

The old Indian fell silent. They had arrived at his destination, and Reverend David Young stopped to let him out of the car. They never met again. Reverend Young died in 1976, so he did not live to see the further fulfillment of this remarkable prophecy.

White Feather spoke of the events that mark the transition from the Fourth World to the Fifth World; events that were foretold over one thousand years ago. The final event being the return of Pahana, the lost White Brother of the Hopi, **from the stars**, that will bring the missing piece of a sacred tablet that is now kept by Hopi elders in a secret place. The following are interpretations of the events described by White Feather:

The first sign that was prophesied was the arrival of white-skinned men that resembled Pahana. But unlike Pahana, these white men lacked integrity and took the Hopi land with thunder. He then positioned his arms as if holding a rifle and pointed the imaginary weapon at me. Then as if pulling the trigger he said the thunder of gunfire from the guns of the white man fulfilled the prophecy that had been made four hundred years before the arrival of Columbus.

The second sign described spinning wheels filled with voices. The elder said that the white men with guns of thunder prepared the way for white settlers in covered wagons with spoke wheels, spinning their route across the plains. And those spoke wheels carried the voices of pioneers moving west. This was foretold hundreds of years before their arrival.

The third sign foretold a beast that was similar to a buffalo but with long horns. And the long horned beast will overrun the land. He looked at me and asked if I needed additional explanation.

The fourth sign predicted the land would be crisscrossed by iron snakes. The train made travel cheaper and faster, and the iron snakes are its tracks.

The fifth sign depicted a large spider web that covered the land. A depiction that best illustrates a network of telephone and power lines soon followed the expansion of the white man.

The sixth sign foretold of a network of river stone that makes pictures in the sun. Of course the obvious is the concrete and asphalt highways and the mirages they create.

The seventh sign predicted the sea turning black and causing the death of life. Oil spills. The Transocean rig *Deepwater Horizon* exploded on April 20, 2010. The rig sank two days later and the result was the spilling of as much as 50,000 gallons of oil per day into the Gulf of Mexico. The oil slick is visible from space. And there are plumes of oil one mile deep creating an acute hazard to all marine life. The leak could not have happened in a worse place as the circulation of water on the sea floor in the area is minimal. *Dead Zones* where there is no circulation lacks oxygen and the existence of bacteria. And without bacteria, the oil will not be broken down by natural methods and will remain essentially forever. The oil at the surface is expected to wash ashore along the gulf coast and the eastern seaboard.

The eight sign described the white youth growing their hair long and adopting the ethics of the Hopi; the Hippy movement of the 1960s.

The ninth prophesied a dwelling in the sky that will fall to the earth as a blue star. Soon after the Hopi ceremonies will cease. The Skylab Space Station fell to earth in 1979, and according to eye witnesses appeared to burn with a bluish color on reentry.

The reference to the *white man's battle* against those who possessed *the first light* foretells of a war. And those who possessed the first light are the inhabitants of the Asian and African continents. The weapons used in this war are compared to the atomic weapons testing performed in the American Southwest. Along with the explosive aspect of the weaponry, disease was an added caveat of death and dying.

Another Hopi prophecy warns that nothing should be brought back from the Moon – obviously anticipating the Apollo 11 mission that returned with samples of lunar basalt. If this was done, the Hopi warned, the balance of natural and universal laws and forces would be disturbed, resulting in earthquakes, severe changes in weather patterns, and social unrest. All these things are happening today, could the cause be the Moon rocks?

The Hopi also predicted that when the *heart* of the Hopi land trust is dug up, great disturbances will develop in the balance of nature, for the Hopi holy land is the microcosmic, a holographic, image of the entire planet. Any violations of nature in the Four Corners region, such as coal and uranium mining, will be reflected and amplified all over the Earth.

The Hopi also have prophesied that *Turtle Island* – North America – could turn over two or three times and the oceans could join hands and meet the sky. This seems to be a prophecy of a *pole shift*; a flipping of the planet on its axis. The Hopi call this imminent condition and that of society today *Koyaanisqatsi*, which means *world out of balance...a state of life that calls for another way.*

In 1959, a six-man delegation of traditional Hopi leaders led by the late spiritual leader, Dan Katchongva, traveled to the United Nations Building in New York to fulfill a sacred mission in accordance with ancient Hopi instructions. Because of their prophetic knowledge, the Hopi leaders felt it was time to go east to the edge of their motherland, where *a house of mica*, the United Nations building, would stand at this time, where Great Leaders from many lands would be gathered to help any people who are in trouble.

They were to go when the motherland of the Hopi, and other Indian brothers, were about to be taken away from them. And their way of life was in danger of being completely destroyed by evil ones among the White Men and by some other Indian brothers who were influenced by the White Race. The betrayal of Indian-U.S.A. treaties, land sales, and coal and uranium mining are destroying the Hopi land and its people. And as Hotevilla goes, so goes the planet, and all other peoples and lands, in eventual effect.

According to prophecy, at least one, two or three leaders or nations would hear and understand the Hopi warnings, as *it is told that they too should know these ancient instructions.* Upon hearing the message of the Hopi, they would act immediately to correct many wrongs being done to the chosen race; the Red Man who was granted permission to hold in trust all land and life for the Great Spirit. This prophecy would seem to have failed. Hopi prophecy also declares that the doors of the *Glass House* would be closed to them. This was the case at first, though they have delivered their message to the United Nations Assembly since then:

> *When the Great Leaders in the Glass House refuse to open the door to you when you stand before it that day, do not be discouraged or turn about on the path you walk, but take courage, determination, and be of great rejoicing in your hearts, for on that day the White Race who are on your land with you have cut themselves from you and thereon lead themselves to the Greatest Punishment at the Day of Purification. Many shall be destroyed for their sins and evil ways. The Great Spirit has decreed it and no one can stop it, change it, or add anything to it. It shall be fulfilled!*

Hopi prophecy also tells us that there will be a mass migration of Indians northward from Mexico and Central and South America. This migration will be more than isolated border crossings of desperate people in search of a better lifestyle; it will be led by a 130-year old Indian named Etchata Etchana and will be epic in its magnitude. The movement will come after *the huge fire and explosion* that will create a great need. It will also herald the advent of the True White Brother from the sky.

Hopi prophecy and history are intimately tied to life beyond this planet. On August 7, 1970, a spectacular UFO sighting was witnessed by dozens of people and photographed by Chuck Roberts of the Prescott, Arizona Courier. This sighting occurred after a *UFO calling* by Paul Solem and several Hopi Indians. This sighting was interpreted by some Hopis as being a partial fulfillment of a certain Hopi prophecy given by the Great Spirit Maasau. And inscribed on Second Mesa is a warning of the coming of Purification Day, when the true Hopi will be flown to other planets.

According to Hopi belief, the survivors of the Great Deluge thousands of years ago split up into four groups that moved north, south, east and west. Only one group completed their journey to the North Pole and back under the guidance of a brilliant *star* in which the Great Spirit Maasau traveled. When he landed, he drew a petroglyph on Second Mesa, showing a maiden with the traditional butterfly hair arrangement riding in a wingless, dome-shaped craft. The petroglyph signified the coming Day of Purification when the true Hopi will fly to other planets in *ships without wings*.

# 2012: A SECOND COMING

*"If I become President, I'll make every piece of information this country has about UFO sightings available to the public and scientists. I am convinced that UFOs exist because I have seen one."*
President Jimmy Carter

At their latitude, the !Kung Bushmen of the Kalahari Desert in Botswana describes it as the backbone of night, supporting the heavens and preventing the campfires in the sky from falling at their feet. The Chinese believe it to be a barrier preventing two lovers from meeting. And only with the aid of magpies creating a winged bridge can the two, Vega and Altair meet on the seventh day of the seventh month each year. The Inca describes it as a herdsman following a llama toward a serpent representing their connection to nature and the earth. The Lakota people held in utmost reverence the most mystifying of all heavenly phenomena calling it the pathway of the dead. It is the trail all Lakota people must take when fate overtakes them. The Greeks attribute it to the spraying of Hera's, Queen of Heaven's, milk into the night sky as Hermes was pulled from her nipple. It is still called the Milky Way.

Most Westerners have never seen this awesome sight, or at the very least given it much notice. Atmospheric pollution muddies the skies and cloaks the view of what is essentially the skyline of this part of the Universe. And the wash of artificial light from the cities, towns and campfires dilutes one's resolution even more. Earth's positioning places it in what one would call the suburbs of the Milky Way galaxy. Located on the fringe of the Carina-Cygnus spiral arm, humanity's perspective of the galaxy is edge-on. And there is a cloud of dark cosmic, carbon matter that further veils the core from view. And the core is what the Mayans call the Hunab K'u, which means the mother's womb.

That of which humanity is so intimately connected is cutoff from the senses and yet, there is a gentle and unrelenting tug from something beyond understanding that is calling us to return. This tugging is affecting everyone on the planet, and is increasing with the approach of the end of the calendar.

All things are dynamic. The immobile rock that appears to be motionless is so only because of scale. Peering deeper into its makeup, one finds movement at the molecular level – one finds awareness. And as we watch the heavens one sees movement, and yet the sensation is that the observer is stationary, immobile – this too is an illusion. The solar system of which earth is a part and all things that are on the planet are moving toward a moment in galactic history no living human has ever experienced. Everything has consciousness, and all things are dynamic.

*** 

Sitting under a Tsalam tree, I had been cultured in the mysteries of the Maya. Everything has relevance and nothing is a result of coincidence. It was at that moment something fell from the tree onto my lap. It was a honey locust-like pod. This provided an opportunity for Ekahau, my personal guide, to provide to me even more details of this spiritual place. One of Tsalam's claims to fame is that its bark and heartwood provide local Mayan artisans a reddish, brown dye. Traditionally this dye has been used in dying henequen products such as handbags and hammocks. The dye's exact hue depends on the age of the tree and seasonal weather patterns. The bark can be chipped and stored and the smaller the pieces, the more vibrant the dye. Ekahau then paused in his narrative and I turned toward the temple of Kukulkan. It was bathed with colored light in preparation for the evening presentation. The tourists were scampering about to jockey for a better view. Earlier that day I had climbed the nine-layered step-pyramid and viewed the world of the Maya.

The architecture of the pyramid that the locals call El Castillo is full of symbolism. The symbolism references the importance of a unique calendar in the lives of the Maya. There are four stairways on each side of the structure leading up to the central platform. Each stairway has 91 steps, making the total 364. And with the added step leading to the central platform the total then becomes 365, equal to number of days of the *solar* year. On either side of each stairway are nine terraces. The 18 sectional terraces on each face of the pyramid represents the months of the Mayan solar calendar. On the facing of these terraces are 52 panels, representing the 52-year cycle of the Maya that marks a time when both the solar and religious calendars would become realigned, a time of forgiveness of debt and renewal of faith.

On the staircase of the northern exposure of the pyramid are sculptures of the feathered serpent. Feathers represent the ascension of human consciousness back to its origins while the serpent represents human physical reality. These carvings run down the sides of the staircase and are aligned so that a special effect occurs on the spring and fall equinox. On these two days, the setting sun casts the shadow of the stepped-terraces onto the ramp of the northern stairway, forming diamond patterns. As the sun sets, the patterns created by shadows form a dynamic representation of an undulating snake descending from the central platform. Slowly it descends into the earth symbolizing the connection of the physical with the spiritual, uniting DNA with consciousness.

Quetzalcoatl is a Nahuatl word composed of two separate words; *quetzal* which is a bird of Guatemala that is known for very long green tail feathers that were highly prized and *coatl* which means serpent. The Maya knew this entity as Kukulkan. Kukulkan was a god of much responsibility and wore many hats. He was known for being the god of creation and giver of life, as well as, the creator of the cosmos. He was also the giver of maize. Kukulkan was also known as Quetzalcoatl. And was described as a white man, with a beard, who wore long robes, and who gave a message of love, forbidding the blood sacrifice. Teaching of the One Supreme God, and giving many material things of their culture, such as the calendar.

Having recently viewed a movie that portrayed the Maya as sun-worshipping savages that placed human sacrifice at the center of their culture, I had stood and meditated at the place atop the pyramid where these rituals were purportedly performed. The ending of the movie showed a Spanish galleon docked offshore of a tropical beach and the appearance of white Europeans at the edge of the surf. These conquistadors were portrayed as the saviors of the common Mayan from the barbaric passions of the elite.

Historical records suggest that the Spanish explorer Cortez portrayed himself as the promised return of Quetzalcoatl from the east. Cortez's native mistress, Malinche, served as a translator of language and culture and unwittingly provided the seed for a plan to deceive the inhabitants of the New World. Equipped with superior weaponry, vile deception and in a mockery of his religion,

Cortez obliterated cultures that were equal to that in Europe. What was not accurately told was that the Mayan civilization that was presented in the movie was long gone prior to the arrival of the European invasion. And what were also conveniently spared in the movie were acts of violence committed by the Catholic Church. An example of these acts of violence that were sanctioned by the clergy was the authorizing of the murder of up to nine million women for having intuition, having a gut feeling – that is, practicing witchcraft. And this practice of unbridled control and slaughter continued in the New World.

The Maya were far from being backward or barbaric. Their science, art and agriculture rivaled that of Europe, and in many ways exceeded it. The Maya arose from the Olmec culture. The Olmec were prominent in eastern coastal Mexico between 1200 and 400 B.C., and are remembered for constructing massive earthen mounds, sculpting giant basalt heads, and building large and prosperous cities that existed for hundreds of years. As the Olmec declined, the Mayans ascended to prominence. Historical evidence seems to indicate the presence of a Mayan culture in present day Mexico at least as far back as 1800 BCE, but their greatest influence was exerted between 200 B.C. and 1000 A. D.

The Maya's sphere of influence stretched from the Yucatán Peninsula southward into Central America. The Mayans did not exercise strong administrative control over the empire, but instead developed as a series of largely autonomous city-states. Chichen Itza was one of the largest. Fortified residential cities and meticulously cultivated farmlands were common place. And these cities were connected by what would today be considered a network of interstate highways. Roadways that are called Scabes that were made of limestone crisscrossed the peninsula, and provided a means for travel and commerce. There were 50 such roadways with dimensions of ten to thirty feet in width, and up to sixty miles in length. In addition to a network of connective roads, there was a system of aquifers to provide an adequate water supply to the city-states.

The Maya were the first to develop an advanced writing system in the Americas. Cactus fiber parchment and the dye from the bark of the Tsalam tree were used to chronicle the story of the Maya and fared poorly against the ravages of time, as the heat and humidity slowly erased history. The Spanish censors saw to the destruction of much of the remainder with a more deliberate approach of fire. However, carvings on stone have survived and provide much of what is known today about their civilization. The Coba stelae, for example proves to be somewhat of a Rosetta stone in deciphering Mayan cosmology and the meaning and the end date of the Mayan calendar.

The Mayans were also gifted in science and mathematics. It was the Mayans who independently developed the concept of zero, and Mayan astronomers deduced that a solar year was slightly more than 365 days accurately calculating the additional six hours. The *humane* intellectuals of antiquity were not the *savages* depicted in Mel Gibson's film.

The decline of Mayan civilization was well under way by 1100 B.C.E. The causes are uncertain. Standard anthropological speculation points to warfare, crop failures, and disease as leading possibilities. This pat answer on the surface covers all conventional possibilities, as if answering a multiple choice question with *all of the above*. Europe and the world were experiencing the Dark Ages at this time because of the departure of the demigods, this, too, affected the Maya and their ability to survive. The exodus of the demigods was a worldwide happening. The inability to provide answers and solutions to complex issues gave rise to abject surrender to mysticism. And as Europe struggled with its own brand barbarism, so did the Maya. The society was eroded by its religion, which emphasized human blood. Nobles mutilated themselves to cause their blood to flow onto fabric, which was then burned as an offering.

Ultimately, the practice of the burning of the nobles blood stained fabrics was deemed inadequate and human sacrifice became the norm. The sacrificed individuals had their still-beating hearts cut from their chests. And while still beating, the heart was displayed to the multitude gathered for these spectacles. Often those that were victims of this ritual were the nobility captured in battle. And yet others were volunteers, martyrs seeking to placate the gods.

By the time of the Spanish arrival around A.D. 1520, the Mayans were a starkly diminished civilization. Their great cities were abandoned and the remnants of their population widely scattered. The mysteries the Mayans left behind is intriguing and phenomenal. The grandest of the mysteries is the Mayan calendar. This time keeping system is a combination of several cycles that work together, marking the movement of the Sun, the Moon and Venus. The sacred calendar called the Tzolkin is based on the cycles of the Pleiades, encompassing vast periods of time.

As the earth rotates on its axis, it also wobbles as if it were a spinning top. That is, over time, the true northern star will alternately change from Polaris, as we see it on any given night, to Vega of the distant past. This process is called the precession of the equinoxes and takes 25,625 years to complete a cycle. And the appearance and movement of this star relative to the Mayan Observatories perspective is interesting. The infinitesimally small movement of Polaris over a time period of a thousand years is unremarkable. And yet, the Maya had a complete understanding of the 25,625 year cycle.

The Maya had two calendars. The Tun, which is the divine or prophetic calendar, has 360 days. A variation of this calendar called the Haab which is the civil calendar has 360 days of the Tun plus five bonus days called the *vayeb*. This calendar was used for fiscal purposes such as the timing of paying taxes, because it was based on the local planetary perspective of agricultural seasons. The Tzolkin which has 260 days was considered the astrological or personal calendar. Both the Tun and Tzolkin calendars were designed with a perspective beyond the solar system; an understanding that is more universal in nature. The Gregorian calendar that is used today on the other hand is extremely provincial using the Sun and the Earth exclusively. The Tun did not have as its basis any celestial object; it simply reflected a full cycle of the 360 degrees of a circle. The Tzolkin has as its basis the factors of the numbers thirteen and twenty.

There are thirteen *Intentions* of creation and twenty *Aspects* of creation. The thirteen Intentions represent each day of a thirteen-day calendar week. And the twenty Aspects represent a calendar month in a twenty-month calendar year. And a combination of one Intention and one Aspect defines each day of the Tzolkin calendar. One's birth on a day with a specific Intention and Aspect does not predict one's future it governs it. That is, one lives one's life according to an Intention and an Aspect and that becomes one's destiny. This is because one's birth date is no coincidence. And to serve as a reminder of that destiny, a Mayan's first name is a combination of the Intention and Aspect so that everyone knows that individual's purpose in life. Every Mayan knew their purpose in living and each life had meaning. Reflective in today's Western culture is that of the criminal. Sociologists have concluded that those who commit crimes are those who have identity problems, low self esteem and have no meaningful purpose in living; the Mayans did not have this problem.

The Tun and Tzolkin calendars were represented as interlocking wheels as if the two were a set of gears. The Tun being the larger wheel, or gear, had 360 teeth and the smaller wheel, or gear, is the Tzolkin and has 260 teeth. As the two turn, each combination of unique teeth defined a day. And it takes 52 revolutions for the same originating teeth to match up again.

The night before this reunion of the teeth that marked the beginning, all fires throughout the empire were extinguished. Completely, with no ember was remaining. The next day, the day of the reunion of the original teeth on the calendar wheels, the priest in each city-state lit a ceremonial fire. And from those holy flames, the fires of the empire were reignited. All debts were forgiven as each Mayan started anew with a clean slate as the wheels turned toward the next fifty two year cycle. These acts represented a time of singularity when all things were one and all things were connected, harkening to a time the Maya knew about long before Western scientist.

There were much longer periods of time that were monitored by the Maya. The Long Count is 5,125 years in length. And this represents one-fifth the time for the precession of the equinox, which is 25,625 years in length. The ending of this precession also marks the end of the Fifth Age of the Maya that began August 13, 3113 BC and ends on December 21, 2012.

Calendars are important to a culture with regard to timing and consciousness. That is, if one can be told what time it is, one can be directed as to what to do, and when to do it. Consequently, one can be told what to think. And on what one focuses, one deems important. The Gregorian calendar is constructed from an extremely local perspective, that of the Sun and Earth's movement around it. And to most, that is at a scale that is all-encompassing. And therein lays the sinister aspect of this belief. It is a belief that excludes a much grander perspective.

Just as one is encouraged by modern consumer advertising to focus on the physical aspect of living, and living without consequence, all the while ignoring the spiritual, so does Gregorian time focus one on this life and locality rather than the eternal and universal. The Maya's focus was more extreme. And to ignore this connection is to become what many ancient cultures deem as unconscious. So, what did there calendar measure, time, or something else? A stone in Coba reveals the answer.

An obelisk was discovered near Coba, Mexico in the late 1940s. Lying in the mud for centuries, its unearthing was timely as humanity approached the twenty first century. When the stone was lifted it revealed a wealth of information that proved to be a type of Rosetta stone for deciphering the Mayan calendar. The dimensions of the stone were roughly twelve feet in height and seven feet in width. And the information it contained related consciousness to time.

There are nine layers of the Mayan Step pyramid. And there are nine Steps of the explanation of the Mayan calendar on the Coba stone. Each layer has thirteen sections representing seven periods of light and six periods of dark. The light periods represent times of enlightenment and the dark periods represent times of applying enlightenment. The fifth period of each layer is significant. Other, more ancient cultures had a similar approach to explaining time and history using a seven day creation. The Maya is the most recent and consequently, has fresher information.

Each layer of the calendar focuses on a time frame of galactic history. Each layer starts at a specific time in the past and culminates on the calendar's end date. The first layer starts 16.4 billion years in the past at the time of the Big Bang. Each of the 13 periods represented 1.26 billion years and each had a purpose. The formation of the Universe obviously began in the first period at the time of singularity. And earth's solar system formed in the fifth period. The first single-celled life forms began in the thirteenth. This layer of the calendar is called the Cellular to reflect a significant development; that of consciousness and life it's self. From the Big Bang to the present, Indians making clay pots in the humid jungles of the Yucatan were contemplating vast periods of time, that were later confirmed in the twentieth century. So, with a reading of each layer, one's attention is drawn ever closer to a narrowing period of time. And as the time narrows, consciousness increases as if being drawn in by a vortex.

The second layer of the calendar begins 820 million years in the past and, once again, culminates in the present. Each period of time represents 63.4 million years. This layer is named Mammalian because of the presence of live births.

The third layer of the calendar begins 41 million years ago. Each period represents 3.2 million years. This layer is called the Familiar because of the development of family groups that are associated with primates.

The fourth layer of the calendar begins 2 million years ago. Each period represents 154, 000 years. This layer is called the Tribal because of the development of group cooperation.

The fifth layer of the calendar begins 102,000 years ago. Each period represents 7,800 years. This layer is called the Cultural because this is when organized farming developed.

The sixth layer of the calendar begins 5,125 years ago. The specific date is August 13, 3113 BCE. Each period represents 394 years. This layer is called the National as an ancient king married two cultures to become Egypt.

The seventh layer of the calendar begins in 1755 A.D. Each period represents 19.7 years. This layer is called Planetary with the development of global communications and the invention of the Internet in 1992.

The eighth layer of the calendar begins January 5, 1999. Each period represents 360 days. This layer is called Galactic because of the growing awareness of other worlds and solar systems.

The ninth layer of the calendar begins April 5, 2012. Each period represents 20 days. This layer is called Universal. And the future holds a significant event for those who will bear witness.

Time appears to be speeding up. This is an illusion. Time as a mode of measurement is constant, and it inexorably marches on. And the sensation of speeding up is not with regard to time, it is in fact with regard to creation. More and more stuff is happening in less and less time. And what one can experience today in a 360 day period in the 8th layer would take 19.7 years in the seventh and 394 years in the sixth. And consequently, what one would have experienced in the seventh layer taking 394 years would take 20 days in the ninth layer!

Within the first layer of the calendar, on the fifth period of light, the Solar System was formed followed by 2.6 billion years of cosmic bombardment. Earth's source of water came from the collisions of comets. And a common theme of the Mayan calendar is a provision followed by a need. For life to exist on earth, water was required. The second layer witnessed life on land and subsequently its extinction, for the most part in the fifth period of light. Three percent of all earth bound life forms survived.

In the fifth period of layer three, color vision was developed. And in the fifth period of the fourth layer fire was discovered and used as a tool. Once again, just as a need is presented a provision is supplied, the Ice Age occurred in the next period.

In the fifth period of layer five, art was invented as a means of communication. The intent of the communication was to chronicle information for those to come. This intent and action was the first contemplations and conceptualizations of *future*. On the fifth night, Neanderthal became extinct because of their inability to change. Neanderthal had no concept of future, or planning, and thus had no future.

The realization of the Divine within each of us occurred in the fifth period of layer 6. Christ died and his message that we all have access to the source, without the need for an intercessor, defined each person as worthy, spiritual beings. The fifth night marked the fall of Rome after the exodus of the demigods, and the beginning of the Dark Ages. Once again, the provision was the concept that humanity possesses an internal, guiding light. And this followed by a time of need when each day was dark, bleak and troubling.

The seventh layer is a time of possibilities. From Einstein's theory of Relativity and $e=mc^2$ in 1913 liberating science from Newton's pull, to Sir Edwin Hubble's declaration of an infinite universe in 1924, the fifth period of light created a consciousness that everything is possible. The idea that everything is possible was supported by the conclusion that everywhere does exist. There was a degree of comfort in knowing one was a part of something much grander and indestructible and ongoing. And the fifth dark period marked the beginning of World War II and the atomic bomb, and the possibility of global destruction. Once again, a foundation of hope and encouragement was provided prior to the need when fear gripped the world.

The awareness that all things have consciousness is what is being experienced in the eighth layer. Both animate and inanimate *things* are becoming more revered. Rights were granted to earth's life forms that had once been deemed as expendable. And these rights were afforded protection by civil and criminal laws. And protection of resources that were once considered inexhaustible is now being recognized and preserved. This level of consciousness stems from the realization that the pale blue dot on which all of life resides must live in harmony and balance. Galactic knowledge is increasing exponentially and ethics will define the age.

Layer nine is called the Universal. And life from beyond our planetary experience will be made known. Humanity will know without question we are not alone in the Cosmos. Political leaders of the more prominent nations are already beginning to slowly disclose what is currently known, that earth has been visited for a long time by extraterrestrials. In a speech to the United Nations General Assembly, Forty-second Session, Provisional Verbatim Record of the Fourth Meeting, September 21, 1987, President Ronald Reagan suggested the unbelievable:

> *In our obsession with antagonisms of the moment, we often forget how much unites all the members of humanity. Perhaps we need some outside, universal threat to make us recognize this common bond. I occasionally think how quickly our differences worldwide would vanish if we were facing an alien threat from outside this world...and yet, I ask, is not an alien force already among us?*

NASA astronaut John Glenn representing what one would consider a scientist' perspective explains the government's concern regarding the public's right to know:

*Back in those glory days, I was very uncomfortable when they asked us to say things we didn't want to say and deny other things. Some people asked, you know, were you alone out there? We never gave the real answer, and yet we see things out there, strange things, but we know what we saw out there. And we couldn't really say anything. The bosses were really afraid of this, they were afraid of the War of the Worlds type stuff, and about panic in the streets. So we had to keep quiet. And now we only see these things in our nightmares or maybe in the movies and some of them are pretty close to being the truth.*

Vatican priest Monsignor Corrado Balducci responded to a question posed to him by a reporter. The focus of the question centered on the existence of extraterrestrials and their interaction with humankind:

*That's an interesting point. It's arguable that these beings have been protecting and helping us for a long time. Some people have put forward the hypothesis that some disasters have been avoided thanks to them...*

*...in any case, it's absurd to think that the only form of intelligence is our own. Other intellectual forces, different to the human one and constructed with a different type of structure are not only possible, but extremely probable.*

Ben Rich, former Head of the Lockheed Skunk Works and developer of the F-117A Nighthawk states:

> *We already have the means to travel among the stars, but these technologies are locked up in black projects and it would take an act of God to ever get them out to benefit humanity. Anything you can imagine we already know how to do. There are two types of UFOs – the ones we build, and the ones they build. We learned from both crash retrievals and actual 'hand-me-downs'. The Government knew, and until 1969 took an active hand in the administration of that information. After a 1969 Nixon 'Purge', administration was handled by an international board of directors in the private sector."*

The disclosure of extraterrestrials, not by human proclamation but by public display, will certainly shake what are now the foundations of science, religion, politics and economics. And even though this will mark a beginning of higher consciousness, this will most likely be defined as the end of the world by those whose vision is clouded by ego. Those that were known to the ancient Sumerians as *those who came from heaven to earth* could once again interact with humankind as they did some 500,000 years ago. And those that the Hopi await that will take them to other worlds in *ships without wings* may make their appearance. And their *second coming* will mark a new beginning.

# THE D-WORD

*Human salvation demands the divine*
*disclosure of truths surpassing reason.*
Thomas Aquinas

Disclosure is constantly happening, whether one realizes it, or not. Prior to the event that jolted me to awareness, far too often I did not recognize, or acknowledge that anything was being communicated to me. And as I have described many times in this writing, what one experiences, observes, or senses is more times than not a tutorial in existing as a participant. One cannot obsess about the past, as I had done far too often. Reliving decisions and missed opportunities can rob one of life's lessons. And unbridled focus on the future has similar results, creating a daydreamer's existence. Recounting an event in my life where a close friend made a passing reference to his mother purchasing burial plots for the entire family as being morbidly comical, I later learned that he was a reaching out. It was a call for help that later resulted in suicide. Another incident was a client that had been extremely difficult to please. This displeasure continued for years and one day, on a Friday, she apologized for the grief she had caused. And she said she could not leave my office until I had forgiven her. I later learned she committed suicide the day after our meeting. The note she left was short and contained one sentence; suicide may be as much a way in, as a way out. Although these examples are extreme, I felt as though I should have recognized these patterns, and did not. As a result, I am much more sensitive to what others may term coincidence.

Learning to recognize disclosure is as much an exercise in not over rationalizing as much as it is being aware of other's needs, or desires, to be forthcoming. That is, there are times when what is communicated is all that can be stated, and the method of communication is what is available. For example, thousands of people have read Homer's Iliad and Odyssey and its accounting of a mythical city named Troy. Heinrich Schliemann in the 1870s interpreted literally the existence of the city from the writing and followed the descriptions provided in the text to area where excavations revealed what was once thought to be myth. Schliemann did not succumb to over rationalization and believed the message. Most of us have a press-conference mentality that everything noteworthy and important is a scheduled news event. There is a belief that the release of information that is important is presented in a particular form and fashion. With bright lights and the credibility of a trusted news anchor, or an elected official, or a knowledgeable scientist or economist, anything that is communicated from these sources has to be the truth. And, conversely, if these same entities are silent on any given subject, that information either must not exist, or lacks credibility. With the above examples, I suppose I was waiting for both of my suicidal friends to state the obvious and request a special meeting to discuss their feelings. They did, I just didn't listen.

In the previous chapter, the scenario was presented that there could be a public disclosure on a scale that most, if not all, would comprehend. And then again, that public disclosure would have to be recognized and not overly analyzed and explained away by cultural prejudice. In fact, public disclosure of the existence of extraterrestrials and the evidence of artifacts throughout the solar system exist. It is public, and has been for a long time. What is lacking are press conferences and news anchors providing sound bites. Those that are releasing this information do so in a routine manner that escapes the attention of the rank and file. Military and political leaders, influential civilians, even Hollywood have been instruments in preparing the way for disclosure. And it seems there is a group of individuals that has existed from the time of WWII to the present that are not only privy to, but are instrumental in the dissemination of this information.

On December 9, 2009, two events that are seemingly unconnected, except for the timing, occurred over northern Norway and Moscow, Russia. These two events coincided with the visit of President Obama to Oslo, Norway to accept the Nobel Peace Prize. In the skies above northern Norway, a Russian test missile was launched purportedly as a sign of strength and posturing as the American President arrived in Scandinavia. The missile was intercepted by what some have called a torsion beam. The torsion beam slowed the speed of the missile from 12,000 mile per hour to that of a small prop plane. And in doing so, the torsion beam spun the missile in a tight spiral causing the fuel to escape in concentric rings of escaping gas. The missile crashed. The origin of the torsion beam is still unclear. There is a facility near the area of the incident that was a Soviet laboratory designed to develop this type of physics. And this type of physics would be akin to the tractor beam concept made popular by the television series Star Trek. Another explanation involves the intervention of a UFO.

A few hours after the missile incident, an object was photographed hovering above the Basilica of Saint Basil the Blessed in Moscow. The object was not widely reported and the release of the image made by two men seemed to be a permitted act by Russian officials. Details of the image and its placement and proportions have survived scrutiny. The shape of the craft is tetrahedral, as if it were a pyramid floating on its side. Speculation by those that research this type of event have resulted in a belief that the UFO was cloaked from normal vision and could be detected only by special camera equipment. The two Russians photographed the object with special equipment. These two events, strange and sci-fi like as it may seem have been observed numerous time. Torsion wave images taken by satellites have documented this happening around the globe. And flying wedges, triangles, or tetrahedrals have been observed worldwide, as well.

A few months after the apparent coincidence of an intercepted missile, an object hovering over Moscow, and President Obama's acceptance of the Nobel Peace Prize, was the announcement made by NASA Administrator Charles Bolden that the new mission of the space agency was to improve Muslim relations. One has to wonder if there were pressures brought to bear to live more peaceably on earth. There are those that may view the four events as separate and distinct, or at the very least, see a pattern involving a couple. And most dismiss any connections, at all, and are waiting on the press, the government, or a gathering of UFOs over the capitals of the world to provide the disclosure.

Another example of disclosure involves an elected official. President Kennedy announced on May 25, 1961 that the United States would send a man to the moon and return him safely to earth. And that this would be achieved by the end of the decade. Many believe that his motive was to out race the Soviets in the development of technology. With the existence of the Cold War and the vestiges of McCarthyism, it was an easy rationalization.

And certainly the political environment was such that the passion to beat the Russians was ample if fueling and funding the initiative. But, why would the President in a time of economic down turn allocate incredible amounts of money and effort to send a human to the moon when human rights and employment were a more pressing problem.

The Apollo program was strategically implemented by the Kennedy Administration. The placement of key NASA facilities in the South in Texas, Louisiana, Mississippi, Alabama and Florida provided an economic and technological stimulus for a region of the country with an agricultural past. Added to that the requirement that federal government regulations required the hiring of minorities and Kennedy had set in motion the resolution of two social ills; the economy and civil rights. And if that were the end of the story, the revolution in technology and the aggressive move toward racial equalities would have been enough to have assured Kennedy's place in history. Since the Release of Information Act, additional information has been discovered, however. What was the real reason for the moon missions?

Documents that were released under the Freedom of Information Act revealed photographs taken from a US satellite that was built and deployed to provide surveillance of the Soviet Union. This surveillance recorded the landscape of something else, however. The images taken from this spy satellite prior to the announcement of the Apollo Mission were exclusively that of the lunar surface. The post-discovery rationale was that it was easier to secure funding for defense than it was for space exploration, or in this case, confirmation of extraterrestrials. So, build a spy satellite under the guise of photographing an imminent threat and then use it how one will. Other disclosed documents suggest that President Kennedy was made aware of the existence of objects on the moon that were considered artifacts. Things left there by life forms. And the interest of the United States, and other nations was not to simply fly to moon; it was to retrieve artifacts of intelligent design.

For those that are suspicious consider this, President Kennedy had approached the Premier of the Soviet Union, Nikita Khrushchev to persuade him and his country to share the cost and the rewards of the space program. That is, work in unison to fly to moon and safely return. The Cold War being what it was, the idea of any partnership with the communists would have been farfetched and borderline treasonous. Kennedy, on the other hand, knew what was on the moon would make earth a smaller place politically, and perhaps bridge many ideological differences. Khrushchev dismissed the offer initially, and then agreed to Kennedy's offer. After the agreement had been made, President Kennedy was assassinated a few days later on November 22, 1963. A few weeks later, Premier Khrushchev was imprisoned and essentially never heard from again. With one man dead and the other imprisoned and broken, the Cold War lasted another twenty years. Many conspiracy theories exist for both incidents. But, the common ground each man shared was that both were in agreement to disclose the existence of alien or human artifacts on another world. And the reasons for extreme measures by a select group were to either escalate the Cold War, or prevent the disclosure of contact with an alien race.

Arthur C. Clarkes' writing that is titled; <u>2010 The Year We Make Contact</u>, describes the discovery of a tetrahedral object on the moon by astronauts. The pyramid-shaped object is surrounded by a force field. And when the force field is broken by the explorers, an alarm, so to speak, is tripped. The harmonic signal is then sent to the creators of the object to signal humanity's readiness to be contacted. Contact is defined when humans discover the artifacts of an alien race. Kennedy, Khrushchev, and others knew these artifacts exist. Similar areas of interest regarding alien artifacts exist throughout the solar system. The pyramids and the face located in area on Mars named Cydonia have intrigued many for years.

An extensive number of scientists and researchers can be listed that have chronicled volumes that support the existence of alien artifacts: John C. Hoagland, Michael Cremo, and Graham Hancock to list a few. What is not so obvious are the number of science fiction writers and movie makers that seem to have a special insight. Steven Spielberg, George Lucas, Arthur C. Clarke, and many more have seemingly prepared for the way to disclosure. Too many story lines of the past are now becoming the factoids of the present and few make the connection.

On May 12, 1962, General Douglas MacArthur addressed the Corp of Cadets at West Point stated:

> *You now face a new world, a world of change. The thrust into outer space of the satellite, spheres and missiles marked the beginning of another epoch in the long story of mankind - the chapter of the space age. In the five or more billions of years the scientists tell us it has taken to form the earth, in the three or more billion years of development of the human race, there has never been a greater, a more abrupt or staggering evolution. We deal now not with things of this world alone, but with the illimitable distances and as yet unfathomed mysteries of the universe. We are reaching out for a new and boundless frontier. We speak in strange*

*terms: of harnessing the cosmic energy; of making winds and tides work for us; of creating unheard synthetic materials to supplement or even replace our old standard basics; of purifying sea water for our drink; of mining ocean floors for new fields of wealth and food; of disease preventatives to expand life into the hundred(s) of years; of controlling the weather for a more equitable distribution of heat and cold, of rain and shine; of space ships to the moon; of the primary target in war, no longer limited to the armed forces of an enemy, but instead to include his civil populations; of ultimate conflict between a united human race and the sinister forces of some other planetary galaxy; of such dreams and fantasies as to make life the most exciting of all time.*

Certainly General MacArthur was privy to what President Kennedy, and others knew. How much disclosure does one need?

# THE TWINS

*This life's dim windows of the soul*
*Distorts the heavens from Pole to Pole*
*And leaves you to believe a lie*
*When you see with, and not through, the eye.*
*William Blake*

If one can see the miracle of a single flower clearly, one's whole world would change. And my experience the past seven years has been a continuous blooming in awareness. Coincidence has been replaced by divine design, and the emotion of fear that was the source of all of my decisions has been replaced by a much nobler one of love. One is always where one needs to be, at exactly the moment that is required of them, to experience an opportunity in increased awareness. And one's inner voice and higher calling creates a pathway of enlightenment as it has with me since the tragic death of my Mother. All in all, there is an overwhelming sense of gratitude for all that has been experienced. And yet I feel a sense of uneasiness, an urgency to prepare for what would be a natural occurrence from a galactic perspective, but would constitute an upheaval at the local, planetary level.

There is a thought; a message that is as much a calling as anything else, that is constantly with me and is twofold. The primary question is why are they returning? Why are *those that came from heaven to earth* that the Sumerians, the Maya, the Hopi and essentially every ancient culture of earth has chronicled returning on a specific date? On a date that these ancient cultures all agree. And in addition to that, why is there a profound need that has recently been made known to me to return to what would be considered the basics in living?

An overwhelming desire to preserve relationships, to preserve resources, to preserve integrity, to preserve ties to the spiritual has replaced self-serving pursuits of pleasure and gain at the expense of others. And as both a symbolic and a practical act of reverence, the calling to become more cooperative with the earth by creating interdependencies with nature as opposed to ego has become my evangelism. The meaning of which is that the individual is more important than a process, or an outcome. And I have learned that both personal and business results are more long lasting with this understanding. It is the difference in living the rules as opposed to following the rules. The former is an existence of acceptance and belonging, a feeling as if one has arrived at a destination. And the later is as one of searching and longing, a feeling of restlessness that one has no place to call home.

Hopi cosmology and the origins of the universe attribute the world's formation to a set of twins: Poqanghoya and Palongawhoya. They were independently responsible for making the earth solid and for sending a sound, a resonance through the earth, to activate vibratory centers that are a part of earth's axis. After the completion of these tasks, each took a position at the North and South poles. If either were to leave their positions, earth would experience a great upheaval.

To the Hopi, as it is with all ancient cultures, all things are connected. The earth's well being is tied to humankind. We affect the state of the world by both our physical and emotional activity. All of humanity was given a set of instructions, a *life map*, that if followed would maintain a spiritual balance. And if the *life map* is abandoned, and ancestral traditions are forsaken, and people adopt lifestyles that promote personal again, and pleasure at the expense of others, this will have an adverse, visible effect on the natural world. That world that is *out of balance* with divine instructions is called *Koyaanisqatsi*.

\*\*\*

If one were to view the earth from space, it is easy to see that the continents could fit together as pieces of a jigsaw puzzle. Two hundred years ago, Benjamin Franklin hypothesized that Africa and South America were once joined. Science has confirmed that union. 20 million years ago the two continents were one. What caused the separation also provides evidence of Poqanghoya and Palongawhoya leaving their positions. This is called polar shift.

A pole shift refers to the Earth's magnetic field reversing its polarity. North becomes South and South becomes North. This event occurs on a regular basis over time; geologic time. The interval between shifts averages 250,000 years. During the Crustaceous Period, the time of the appearance of flowers, the earth maintained a constant polarity for 30 million years which is considered extreme. The last pole shift took place 790,000 years ago, causing some scientists to believe we're due. While others speculate a reversal is already underway. Scientists have recorded a reduction in the earth's magnetic strength by 10% within the last 150 years. This is believed to be evidence of a current pole shift. This phenomenon is recorded in *new earth*.

The Mid-Atlantic Ridge is a 6,000 mile underwater mountain range. From a point near Bouvet Island at the southern end to a point 207 miles south of the North Pole, the mountain range is more than an uplifted series of peaks, it is a spreading center. At a spreading center such as the one represented by the Mid-Atlantic Ridge, *new earth* is created as volcanism pushes magma toward the surface. When the magma reaches the surface it becomes lava. And as the lava cools, the ferrous material solidifies. And the magnetic property of the ferrous material in the newly formed rock mirrors the polarity of the earth. The polarity of the newly formed crust is constant and provides a historical record of Poqanghoya's and Palongawhoya's positions.

There are alternating bands of new crust that chronicles the flipping of earth's polarity. And the greater the distance from the central ridge one looks the further back in time one goes. One of these bands represents a time the Hopi described when the Third World came to an end. The surface of the earth was destroyed. As the belief avows, the guardians of the poles, the twins Poqanghoya and Palongawhoya, left their positions and caused the icecaps to melt, the continents to shift, strange weather patterns to develop. And the accumulative result was an ice age. The earth's magnetic poles shifted polarity, and the world reversed its rotation. The sun then rose in the west and set in the east. And when the twins returned to their polar positions, the earth stabilized. It was then the humans emerged from the safe place provided by Taiowa with the instructions to go forth and multiply and be grateful. And the absence of gratitude would mean corruption exist.

Polar shift happens. And one is currently underway and will also coincide with another phenomenon; the completion of a galactic cycle which is the precession of the equinoxes. There is much movement in the cosmos. Everyone knows the earth rotates. And we are all familiar with the orbits of the nine planets of the solar system. Some of us understand the spiraling movement of the Milky Way. But there are very few that understand that the galaxy has an equator. And the movement of the earth aligns with that galactic equator at a regular interval. And completion of that cycle of 26,625 years will occur on December, 21, 2012.

*\*\**

There is much written about theories regarding how and what generates the magnetic field of the earth. Still, there are many more unanswered questions than there is understanding, which is unnerving. And when the subject is discussed, there is little consolation. There are those scientists that have linked extinctions of the past with polar shift. And none speculate, other than to offer no comment, on what one might expect with the tandem of a polar shift and the alignment of earth's position with the galactic equator. So, from official sources no response is a response. And as history has proved time, and again, we elect leaders who feel compelled to protect us from ourselves.

The current explanation for the magnetic field is that there is a solid core that rotates at the center of the earth. And it is surrounded by an iron-like liquid. And on top of that is earth's crust. So, a rotating core that is separated from the surface by a liquid that has its own movement creates what is called a dynamo. A dynamo is motor that generates power.

As the earth passes through the electrostatic field of the sun, its liquid core recharges a bit. This recharging is minimal. And far more energy is lost than is generated. And just a battery loses power over time, so does the earth. Scientists have estimated that the magnetic field has been reduced by as much as 60% over the past 2,500 years. This field of energy protects earth from solar radiation. So, there comes a point, when in a few decades, the percentage will drop to a critical level and earth will become exposed to a bombardment of radiation unless something remarkable occurs.

The reversal of polarity, the shifting of the poles, in effect recharges the battery, so to speak. As we speculate what may happen to life on earth when this happens, the ancients, from the Egyptians to the Hopi understand the consequences all too well. Encoded in their history and knowledge was a comprehension of galactic cycles that escapes modern science. When the polarity is reversed on a motor, it spins in the opposite direction.

The earth's reversal in rotation as a result of a polar shift is a tale of two cities. The first tale is of one that preserves life. This means that at the equator the speed of rotation relative to the sun is approximately 1,000 miles per hour. If the reversal in rotation were sudden, one would be flung about as would most things. Radical shifting of water and land masses would create conditions of Biblical proportions. And if it were gradual, the length of a day would change affecting all aspects of life and living. The shifting of land and water masses would also occur. And not to be overlooked, commerce and standards of living which are taken for granted would cease, either gradually, or in the twinkling of an eye. And as severe as the two alternatives may seem, life would still have an opportunity to survive and multiply.

The second tale is one of destruction and extinction. If there is no polar shift, the magnetic field would continue to diminish and that would cause complete extinction of life on earth. The sun emits a steady stream of ionized gases. These gases travel toward the earth at speeds approaching 900,000 miles per hour. The Earth's magnetic field shields it from much of the solar wind. When the solar wind encounters Earth's magnetic field it is deflected like water around the bow of a ship. A weakened, or absent magnetic field would permit the solar radiation to affect everything from public health and bird migration to massive electrical storms and increased radioactive heating. The ultimate consequence would be complete extinction.

The coordination of the spectacular events of polar shift and earth's alignment with the galaxy's equator is eventful. Earth's magnetic force is weakest at the equator. And the Milky Way's magnetic force is the same, weakest at the galactic equator. So, as earth is experiencing its effect of polar shift, it will be aligning its equatorial plane with that of the galaxy and the magnetic field of the Milky Way cannot offer any support, so to speak. As it goes, the coupling of these two events may create conditions for a perfect storm.

*\*\**

My questions still remain. Why are *those that came from heaven to earth* returning at a time that seems to be wrought with peril? Is their mission to observe, or to intervene? Are those that Sumerian cosmology states that genetically engineered the human species coming to witness the destruction of their handiwork? Or, are they planning to assist in a way they have possibly done so many times before?

And does the Hopi admonishment that the land that will be preserved is the third mesa of the Four Corners of Arizona? Does this mean that there are places that are safer than others? My intuition tells me to trust the ancients. And it has been consistent with my experience that when I have a need to know I should go to the source. And that is often those that were taught by entities that came from places called Nibiru, the Pleiades and beyond the backbone of the night.

When I consider what I have learned about one's place in this field of energy that Max Planck called the Mind of God, I am reminded of Neville, a visionary from the island of Barbados, he said,

> *Man's chief delusion is his conviction that there are other causes (in creation) other than his own state of consciousness.*

And it is then the mystery becomes clearer.

As what was mentioned earlier, hologram is a word created from a Greek term *holos* and *gramma* which means the whole picture. And the smallest piece of a hologram contains a complete representation – a whole picture – of the entire image. Modifying one aspect of hologram changes all representative images, both small and large, immediately. And the matrix may be best described as a hologram of existence as we know it. What is done at the local level by human intent then suggests that all of creation mirrors that change. So, change at any level does not have to travel any distance, or take any time to change the whole, because it is one.

As Hopi cosmology suggests, the world's formation is the result of the efforts of a set of twins; Poqanghoya and Palongawhoya. One was responsible for making the earth solid and the other was responsible for making the five vibration centers of earth's axis resonate. This so called *fable* is the answer to my questions.

*Those that came from heaven to earth* are not coming to witness a disaster, or to assist with an evacuation, as some have suggested. They are coming to participate in what may be best described as a graduation, a transition of humankind from a lower level of consciousness to a much higher one. The creation of the earth by the *twins* represents the obvious. One twin making the earth solid is the spirit becoming flesh. And becoming flesh has as its benefit the opportunity for the spirit to experience creation. To feel! And the freedom to feel opens the door to pursue noble intentions, or not. And the other twin's activation of the five vibration centers of the earth's axis represents the chakras of the human body, and the physical experiencing a spiritual existence. And the reference to polar shift is humankind's deviation from the *life plan* – a flip flopping of values, so to speak. And this is a result in not choosing noble intentions which causes a world out of balance called *Koyaanisqatsi*. Ignoring the spirit's need to experience the tangible and the tangible's need to be connected to the spirit is confusion. And that causing what is in effect an end of the world for the unconscious, which is a *shift* from a possession-based existence to a conscious-based existence. And conversely, those that have recognized and have accepted that tug to return to an existence based on the spiritual represents a new beginning for them, a new level of consciousness.

Often the word *World* does not mean earth. It refers to the existence that is created by each person as a result of cognitive depictions of reality. This refers to what one thinks and to one's body which is said to contain the entire universe. This holographic reality is such that as the Hopi say, "What happens in Hotevilla happens to the world" means what happens within a person is reflected in all of creation.

So, the supposed question still exists. If what we collectively think affects the physical world does that imply that humans ultimately control what happens as the Mayan Calendar ends? Do we permit in our lives a higher level of consciousness, or do we consent to a more tragic ending. Either way, it is time for humanity to transition.

Life on earth has experienced many transitions. Looking back to predict the future is a fractal approach to anticipating what we may become. Evolution happens. Not as Darwin suggested as a chaotic series of happenstance where a stronger life form exerts its will over a lesser. Nor does evolution happen randomly without design; there is a consciousness to evolving. Just as experiments have shown where toxic agents were introduced to the environment of simple life forms and their ability to immediately, so to speak, adjust their DNA to survive, so it is nature. Life finds a way, consciously.

Consciousness begins at the simplest level of existence. In 1953, DNA was discovered by James Watson and Francis Crick. This discovery led many to believe that the foundation of life had been discovered. And this belief held fast for 40 years. In 1990, the Human Genome Project led by James Watson sought to patent the design and components of human DNA to market medical interventions. The project was deemed less than successful when the discovery was made that humans possessed the same number of genes as that of roundworms. So, there was something more that defined the differences in life forms, rather than the number of genes each own.

A post Human Genome discovery chronicled by many publications, and one that donned the cover of Time magazine dated January 18, 2010; suggested life has control of its DNA. Epigenetics has demonstrated that the cell membrane, the lining, coordinates the cell's activities and existence by relaying information of its environment to the DNA. The DNA modifies the instructions it produces to reflect the cell's environment. The cell membrane then communicates key data to other cells of its status. This lining, this connection to the outside world, is what affects the instructions produced by the DNA, and in effect, manages the life of the cell.

Life on earth has maintained a constant level of existence punctuated by bursts of development. The first life forms were single-celled Prokaryotes. The size of this single-cell entity was limited due to the restrictions the cell membrane can grow before becoming weak and bursting. And with restrictions on size, there were limits to consciousness. The combined surface area of a membrane can be compared to the brain and its surface area. This represents the first leap in the existence of life on earth.

The second leap, the Eukaryote phase, represents the collection of cells that grouped together. The close proximity of the cells improved their survival. Huddling together, each could maximize their size without endangering the lining. Pressing close together, a sister cell could reinforce the lining of other cells and thus the awareness of each individual cell increased.

The third leap represents the Multi-cellular level. The collection of cell within a common membrane compounded the consciousness of the entity. With each cell sharing the economies of scale created by sharing a common lining, the beginnings of intercellular communication began. Now, consciousness and awareness was a shared experience.

The fourth leap is our current existence, cells sharing a common existence, with the added caveat of specialization. Each cell has a job, whether the cell is specialized to be bone or muscle, nature has orchestrated the cooperation of consciousness to become what we know today. One's body is fifty trillion cells, with specialization, working as individuals for the common good. And this orchestration and cooperation serves as a metaphor for the future.

So that brings us to the next step, the anticipated step of humanities' next level of consciousness. If our heritage is that of a single cell with limited awareness, and then that of a collection of cells with a shared awareness, then the next step is to recognize humanity as a single *cell* of a much larger existence. Acting as individuals for a common good, life as we have known it will come to an end. And a greater existence awaits humankind as specialized members of a higher calling. And this will be achieved by cooperation, not competition.

# IN MEMORY: THE LENTEN MOON

*The mother's heart is the child's schoolroom.*
Henry Ward Beecher

Myrna Sue Carroll died on the afternoon of the full moon prior to Easter; the Lenten Moon. The early Christians used this astronomical occurrence to mark the beginning of a time fasting and prayer; a season spent in mournful respect for the death of Christ. This time of solemn devotion and sacrificial lifestyle continued until the next full moon; the Egg Moon. The Egg Moon marked the end of the mourning and fasting period and signaled the beginning of spring and new growth; a new beginning, a rebirth.

My time of mourning and self denial began on the day of mother's death; my Lenten Moon. And my period of solemn devotion and singularity continued until I experienced my new beginning; my Egg Moon on the day of accountability. On that day I called heaven and earth to stand before those who had with reckless abandonment acted wantonly against my mother. Their admonishment: When given the option of life or death chose life that we all may live. It was not an act of vengeance; the infliction of punishment in return for a wrong committed; a vicious retribution. It was a reckoning; a settlement of a debt; a simple reconciliation of how and why.

I am my mother's child; a life that was produced by her body. Although, she is not with me, I feel I am the fruits of her labor. This struggle has caused me to come to the realization that the true womb of a mother is her heart. And her children are reborn daily unto her good works. If that is true, I'll have many rebirths, scores of days to live on this earth to honor her and her good works. I owe it to that life that lives on in the hearts she left behind, and when you think of it that way, to do that is not really to die. And I finally have reason to smile, and I hope mother is smiling, too.

I will see her again.

# AFTERWORD

*The day science begins to study non-physical
phenomena; it will make more progress in one decade
than in all the previous centuries of its existence.*
Nikola Tesla

The Lenten Moon chronicled the tragic events that caused the
death of my Mother. The tale is typical of one who is looking
for answers, from every source except *The Source*. It is filled with
hurt and disappointment, deceit and arrogance and what seems
to be from the spiritually unconscious perspective eternal and
irreversible decisions. It is a dark and bleak saga of death and
dying.

The Egg Moon gives an account of a select number of
interventions. Interventions whose source is from that higher voice
within each of us. And interventions that has as its modality any
and every aspect of one's senses. With every turn, enlightenment
happened. And the lessons learned is that coincidence is a fable,
a Western invention to explain why remarkable things happen in
our lives when orchestration seems to be astonishingly timely. It is
a type of free-pass for those who ignore the obvious to move on to
what can be measured and tested. Scientists and clergy seem to err
on the side of thinking deeply, instead of thinking clearly. And far

too little credit is attributed to what is a result of the spoken word. Hermann Hesse, a German-Swiss poet, writer and painter said:

> *Everything becomes a little different as soon as it is spoken out loud.*

And the spoken word that is the result of heart-felt intention is the mechanism for change.

Conscious Language will guide one's steps toward making a talk one can walk. What we say is a result of what we think – that is obvious. But what may be not so obvious is how what we say not only affects one's actions; it interacts with the matrix in which we exist. This field of energy is a mirror of our intent and reflects one's thoughts into existence, creating a life of abundance, or lack.

# CONCLUSION

*Knowing others is wisdom, knowing yourself is Enlightenment.*
Lao Tzu

The apparent coincidence of fallen angels, found books, a single word, chance meetings, strange places, guardian angels and new acquaintances were orchestrations of natural laws. There are some that would describe these natural laws as divine; to me the two are the same. And even though what was chronicled in this book is but a fraction of that which was experienced, what was learned is secondary to living one's questions. Experience is the master. Ancient traditions has it that the teacher will appear when the student is ready to learn. And of course, the ancients were correct. When that blending of readiness and opportunity exist, the results can be life changing and is the ultimate source of wisdom. In retrospect, the opportunities for learning experiences had always been there, throughout my life. And it was the unawareness of how I work as a conscious entity that placed obstacles along my pathway.

The obstacles were of my own making. Reflecting on the happenings before and during my experience it is now easy to see that I was the major contributor to my confusion. There were times when I acted childishly expecting others to pull me from my quagmire. Or, I felt resentful I was not allowed to sit at the adults table, so to speak, and take charge of my life. There were other times I knew what to do and what was best for me and I simply compromised for convenience sake to take a path of least resistance. And there were times after having negotiated the childish influences and having resisted the temptation to prostitute my standards, I found myself over rationalizing a circumstance and deciding the effort is not worth the price. The sabotaging of my life's calling by not allowing myself to act appropriately created in me a victims mentality. There were times when I felt being happy and successful were for those better equipped, or more fortunate. Carl Gustav Jung named these characteristics as the four survival archetypes. Caroline Myss described these archetypes as the four legs of a table. And if the four are not tended to and are not aligned the table will wobble, as does everything on the table. And for a long, long time my life was anything but stable.

The realization that these archetypes are enabled by my emotions was a revelation. There are shadow and light aspects of these archetypes. The shadow aspect is what one would consider a negative influence. The light aspect is the opposite. One does not have to surrender to either. There is freewill in one's decision. So, when a dark aspect suggest that one should sellout their principles and make an extreme compromise, for example, one can recognize the dark characteristics and do the opposite. Or, if a light aspect suggests a course of action, one can recognize those beneficial characteristics and take the advice. So, as I have learned, my first action to any given scenario is to first assess the influences my survival archetypes are providing, and second how am I enabling them. As a result, I have learned to think more clearly.

Learning to think clearly instead of deeply often means shedding the preconceptions of Western thinking. The pressure to conform to the tenets of the prevailing belief system means to accept scientific explanations as gospel. Far too often one commits an act of apostasy when a hypothesis from a credentialed authority is questioned. Science is a tool, an extremely valuable tool, one that has made our lives better in many ways. But it is nothing more. And when it is elevated to a status where it is superior to its creator then one has to ask the question: What is more important than the brush, or the artist.

Conversely, western religious thought is largely one dimensional. The value placed on tradition and ritual is extremely important, but it is not understood why it is essential. Prayer is largely misunderstood. And physical explanations for spiritual questions are often discarded by a pious haughtiness that keeps one in a dark age of confusion. The confusion stems from a lack of understanding of the role of human emotion in creation. One always gets what one prays for; so the question then becomes: For what is one praying?

Intuitively, one might entertain the thought that the union of the two belief systems would create a hybrid way of thinking that would produce complete answers. The truth is both religion and science are fallen aspects of a much higher existence. And enlightenment has as its genesis the realization that each person is both the question and the answer; as if each individual is a part of that which one seeks. So, it is not a blending of any belief systems, nor is it alchemy of ideologies, it is a matter of stillness. Stopping, listening and thinking clearly. What one needs to know is given. Where one needs to be is where one is. When one needs to be is now. Why one needs to be is one calling. And when these happen, it is the ultimate modality of existing and giving.

We are all connected. And as humanity moves toward a time predicted by the ancients, a collective consciousness is becoming more pronounced. Even those of us that are considered spiritually unconscious sense a change. And those of us who are more sensitive to the spiritual see an unveiling. Disclosure is happening. Piece by piece, information is divulged. From Winston Churchill's recently released documents of a close encounter between a UFO and a RAF bomber that happened in the skies above war torn England to the Vatican's proclamation that extraterrestrials will be allowed the rite of baptism, acceptance of what was once considered the farfetched is becoming the new norm. Churchill's trepidation of public fear and panic and the loss of faith in religion if the world were made aware of the visitation are being replaced by awareness that there is much more to this world, galaxy, universe and dimensions to experience.

It seems as though time is speeding up. Time seems to be passing much faster now than it did in the past. And when the subject is discussed, the reference to this anomaly is not one where the current passage of time is compared to a distant time of one's youth. The observation is made with more recent comparisons; today compared to yesterday, this year compared to the previous. As real as it may seem, this acceleration of time is an illusion. Intuitively, time is a constant, at least in this dimension. As the Mayans understood, it is not a question of time as much as it is a matter of creation. There is more, and more happening, and more, and more to experience each day. All of this without adding more time to each day. What would have taken a generation to experience in the recent past will only take few days as the calendar counts down to December, 21, 2012. This happening is not limited to technology, it encompasses everything. More frequent earth changes, such as extreme weather patterns, earthquakes, volcanic activity, and extinctions. Additionally, increased disclosures, more inventions, more discoveries, more failings of trusted institutions;

everything is affected. A biblical reference to this occurrence of accelerated creation describes it as a time when men's hearts will fail them for fear, and for looking after those things which are coming on the earth. And yet, as Maryanne Williamson said:

> *Our deepest fear is not that we are inadequate.*
> *Our deepest fear is that we are powerful beyond*
> *measure. It is our light, not our darkness that*
> *frightens us most.*

My journey began as a result of fear and grief, both are strong emotions. And emotions were a constant companion. At the beginning of this quest, my Western-tainted raison d'être was to achieve an emotionless state of rational thinking. I was conditioned to think that one doctor is superior to 10,000 praying saints of God, and that one meteorologist is more knowledgeable than any intuitive farmer. And slowly, as the tales of this writing have documented, I learned through experience and what some would call coincidence that emotion is the catalyst for creation. And as the ancients have taught us through the millennia, the web of creation exists as a platform for the software of human intent to operate. What we experience as heartfelt emotion is mirrored in the world.

The experience, the journey, the quest, however one wants to describe it, has resulted in a heightened sense of awareness. Much has been learned, and even more has been experienced. One could even describe it as enlightenment. And if that is in fact the case, if this has caused enlightenment then it would manifest as a need to serve others. And that is what has happened. The Hunter's Moon chronicles the application of what has been learned and experienced to benefit others.

# About the Author

Von Goodwin is a business consultant, personal coach and the author of books and articles revealing the role of the individual in creation. Since 1985 he has worked with individuals to rediscover ancient wisdom to enrich their personal lives. And he has conducted and participated in over 3,000 seminars, workshops, consulting and coaching sessions with companies and staffers to redirect their focus from key performance standards defined by industry to becoming more aware of the value of collective consciousness. In addition to those appearances, Von has been the featured presenter at several universities imparting the insight of the ancients to the students of the present. He has been a pioneer in breaking down barriers of limiting bureaucracy replacing them with a vision of possibilities.

# About the Artist

Cover Design:

David King creatively captured the essence of this writing in illustrating growth in the most unexpected place. Portraying the detail of a sprout pushing its way through the moon's dry crust, and the added symbolism of the Pleiades constellation floating mysteriously high above is elegant and relevant. This skillfully constructed methodology represents his intent to emphasize an obvious spiritual connection one may find at one's feet and an unsuspecting intellectual enlightenment one may find from above. David has designed many works for both commercial and private use. He resides in Birmingham, Alabama and may be contacted at dk0828@gmail.com.